"Terry McGuire's insights into how reflecting on our Judaic Christian heritage can contribute to ministry formation is a gift to todays' Catholic health care leaders. He traces the roots of leadership from Moses in the Old Testament to Paul's conversion, through the teachings of Teresa of Avila and the example of Cardinal Bernardin. He guides his readers (and students) to reflect on these inspirational leaders and their own lives in order to grow as leaders who can face the challenges of these times."

—*Julie Trocchio, Senior Director, Community Benefit and Continuing Care, Catholic Health Association of America*

"Terry McGuire offers a brief history of acute and long-term care Catholic institutions followed by pointing out saintly models from the past who exemplify what he will urge all leaders to adopt: prayer and reflection as a means to insight and wisdom. Mother Angeline Teresa McCrory, O. Carm. and the well-known St. Teresa of Avila, O. Carm. were key influences in McGuire's plan for ongoing formation, as well as for his life. Women and men in actual and potential leadership roles in Catholic health care institutions would benefit greatly from studying and implementing the experience so thoughtfully laid out by McGuire."

—*Sr. Dolores Zemont, President, Franciscan Sisters of Joliet, Illinois*

"Terry has captured masterfully the beauty in spiritually driven care and its direct relationship to servant leadership in a health care environment. He easily combines his own spiritually-led journey with a fantastic array of other 'wounded healers' who have helped define wisdom leadership. *From Insight to Wisdom* is a comprehensive and deeply inspiring treatise that will serve mission-driven individuals and organizations alike."

—*Raymond Weiss, President and Chief Executive Officer, Grace Lutheran Communities*

"This book is a gem for anyone who seeks to integrate leadership responsibilities with reflective Catholic wisdom. Dr. McGuire's thoughtful discussion includes an insightful historical perspective as well as direct instruction on how to practice the spiritual skill of reflective leadership. I found *From Insight to Wisdom* deeply enriching and recommend it to my colleagues in the mental health, social work, coaching and educational professions."
　　—Kathleen O'Grady, Ph.D., Licensed Clinical Psychologist

"Terry accomplished some wonderful insights into long-term leadership, especially how important reflective leadership is during these stressful times in long-term care! I think it will be a great resource for others who are implementing leadership programs in long-term care."
　　—Sr. Peter Lillian Di Maria, O.Carm., Director, Avila Institute of Gerontology

From Insight to Wisdom

Experiences in Reflective Leadership

Terrance P. McGuire

ISBN: 9781077064683

Imprint: Independently Published

DEDICATION

To Kathleen, Molly, Ross, Nyomi, and Memphis for their continuous encouragement and support, personal challenges, and good humor—all of which enabled me to complete this project.

To all my extended family and friends: Your personal affection and genuineness of heart keeps me going along the path of life.

Thank you.
I love you all!

CONTENTS

ACKNOWLEDGMENTS

To the Carmelite Sisters for the Aged and Infirm and their dedicated staff who minister to the needs of the elderly: I extend my gratitude for the opportunity to work with the team of the Avila Institute of Gerontology in formation and lay leadership development.

To my editor, Shane Cooney, whose skillful wordsmithing and creative examples have brought greater clarity to my work: I'm indebted to him for his understanding and patience in this endeavor throughout this past year.

INTRODUCTION

This book is intended for those presently in positions of ministry leadership, others who are emerging leaders in their organizations, and individuals who work to develop, foster, and advance leadership development. While firmly rooted in the Catholic not-for-profit health care venue, a valuable learning methodology in both theory and praxis emerges from within these pages. To that end, the content is applicable to all leadership learning environments where there is a continuous desire to seek out and find life-changing knowledge.

The basis of this book is my unfolding experience developing and teaching a leadership formation program for lay leaders in Catholic long-term care. This experience took place primarily over the winter of 2016. The development of the program itself was informed by my career of over four decades working as a leader, educator, and consultant in the Catholic health care field. The concepts and processes of reflective leadership were the central elements of the formation program.

Leaders who participate in personal and professional development or other formative experiences that incorporate a reflective method are more grounded in their vision and possess more clarity of purpose when they speak and act on behalf of others. All ministry leaders, including those in Catholic health care, can be enriched by using this reflective method, which draws on human, social, and spiritual aspects of a given situation. It is out of this process that leaders can gain a fresh viewpoint previously unseen by them in their decision-making processes. The use of this skillful method enables them to deepen their own sense of leadership ministry and enrich their lives in their commitment to the service of others in need.

Some of the content in this book is academic in nature, while other parts offer spiritual insights and wisdom from saints both past and present and concludes with the experience of emerging leaders in Catholic long-term care through their summary insights on their experiences and appreciation for the art of reflective leadership. My hope in sharing this experience and my thoughts with you is that you will find the gem that will enable you to enhance your reflective leadership skills and develop them in others.

In the appendix of this book, you will find sample versions of the worksheets I used when teaching the leadership formation program. You may adapt these for your own purposes.

BACKGROUND

In the past one hundred years, the ministry of Catholic health care has experienced numerous changes, both in the way that care is delivered and by whom it is delivered, thus bringing about an overall transformation of the ministry.

In the early formulation of Catholic health care ministry, men and women religious were the pioneers in their congregations to go out and serve the sick and the poor. It was with few resources but a generous heart and a deep Christian commitment that these men and women encountered God in the midst of the suffering of those they tended to day and night. It is from these humble beginnings that the passionate vision of caring for those most in need has arisen.

As health care services in the United States became more prevalent in the mid-nineteenth and early twentieth century, these religious bought homes and later built hospitals with donations from others who saw their good work and experienced their caring presence. Religious sisters and brothers staffed these hospitals and nursing homes and assumed positions of administration in addition to providing hands-on care to patients or residents. Many of these religious communities had multiple ministries and had been previously engaged in education, social service, and health care.

Millions of people and billions of dollars are now committed to serving the sick, elderly, the dying, and many others who experience suffering. The overall population is aware that far more people are elderly and living longer today than in any previous generation.

The United States health care industry, in both acute and long-term care facilities, is facing a challenge like never before in our country. Those who are part of the ever-enthusiastic baby boomer generation have found that by assuming responsibility for their health by routinely eating right, exercising, and sleeping well, while also consciously managing the stress in their lives and keeping active, they are living longer and happily continuing to contribute to society with their knowledge, experience, and acquired wisdom.

The future health care needs of this enormous segment of our society must be addressed with care and compassion.

In 1981, the U.S. Bishops published a letter titled "Health and Health Care: A Pastoral Letter of the American Catholic Bishops," which highlighted the importance of those who care for the physically ill and "restore health and wholeness in all facets of the human community."

MOTHER ANGELINE'S MISSION

In 1929, a distinct religious community of women came into existence in America through the inspiration of Mother Mary Angeline Teresa McCrory. This community came to be known as the Carmelite Sisters for the Aged and Infirm. Mother Angeline had a vision of serving the health care needs of the elderly in facilities that would make them feel that this was truly their home. She wanted to create an environment that reflected the seven aspects—or hallmarks—of her philosophy toward older persons:

1. Having **faith** and confidence in God to serve them as you would Christ himself
2. Maintaining a **vision** to create homelike atmospheres for the elderly at all levels of financial need
3. Being a person of **courage** who is willing to face difficulties with firmness of heart
4. Manifesting **hospitality** and expressing compassion for one another
5. Being a source of **inspiration** by showing that, through your actions, you are filled with joy that will overflow to others

6. Possessing **enthusiasm** and having zeal for your work
7. Demonstrating **leadership** by integrating each of these previous characteristics into the way you lead.

While visionary leaders eventually die, visionary organizations that incorporate their founder's spirit into their work frequently find that their mission and values have become the bedrock from which their ministry is delivered; it grows and flourishes in ever-changing times. Currently, the Carmelite Sisters for the Aged and Inform serve, sponsor or cosponsor nineteen long-term care ministries, where they have adapted to the needs of the times while working ensure the visionary spirit of Mother Angeline is carried on by providing the most up-to-date elder care services. Their mission and core values have withstood the test of time as a cornerstone of their charism.

In 1968, approximately 97% of administrators of Catholic hospitals and nursing homes were religious sisters and brothers. By 2011, that number decreased to 2%. Reasons attributed to this drop in numbers included increased government regulatory systems at both the federal and state levels, which impacted reimbursement and demanded a more complex administrative oversight of services; a shrinking number of religious vocations; and the fact that those who were entering religious communities frequently brought with them management experience from previous work settings and were more attracted to delivering hands-on care instead of assuming a leadership role in the ministry.

Faced with the increasing need for lay leadership within the ministries, the Carmelite Sisters chose to undertake a path that other religious communities in Catholic health care (e.g., hospital ministries) have done. They established a lay leadership formation program entitled "Roots of Caring," which contained heritage and values-based content with the goal that those in management positions chosen to participate in the program would be considered for future senior leadership positions in Carmelite ministries. A unique characteristic of the Carmelite Sisters' ministries is that they are solely focused on long-term care. Therefore, the framework of the formation program needed to be created with this in mind.

1

THE CHANGING HEALTH CARE ENVIRONMENT

"The way up and the way down are one and the same."
Heraclitus of Ephesus, Philosopher

If we come to understand that in many venues of our society, change is the only constant that impacts and influences our lives, we can begin to embrace the saying from Heraclitus.

Health care in the United States continues to undergo monumental change. The impact of the health delivery system has enormous bearing on all the providers of this care and the patients (i.e., those served in acute care) and residents (i.e., those served in long-term care) they are called to serve. Hospitals are the primary provider of acute and emergency care for patients. Nursing homes commonly have mutual agreements in place with hospitals for transferring patients or receiving residents to ensure a continuum of quality care. Any drastic financial changes, in an already complex and brittle system, can ultimately disrupt the health care delivery process.

All health care organizations are facing an unknown future, and in this "in-between time," as agents of change refer to it, health care leaders must stay the course in serving those most in need. In particular, Catholic long-term care ministries receive the majority of their funds through Medicare, Medicaid, and, to a lesser degree, from private pay residents. These facilities have always taken persons who do not have the ability to pay privately and are willing to be reimbursed through the federal government alone. Caring for the poor, aged, and dying is the hallmark of Catholic health care.

Moving forward, leaders of U.S. Catholic health care institutions will be charged with promoting social justice not only through charitable acts, but also by fostering environments that support the dignity, rights, and development of all people. A 1981 Pastoral Letter, "Health and Healthcare," echoes these sentiments. It advocates for Christians to tend to the "wounded," both individually and by virtue of affecting positive change in the social conditions that limit the capacity of mercy and justice.

MOTHER ANGELINE: A VISION OF ST. TERESA

Today's Catholic health care arena is just as challenging, if not more so, than in the previous generations in which Mother Angeline was present. As a young woman, Bridgette McCrory (the future Mother Angeline) was leaving home to enter a religious community. Her local pastor asked her to choose a book from his expansive library. She looked at the books, and she chose *The Life of St. Teresa of Avila*, a woman who influenced Mother Angeline throughout the rest of her life.

She, in her own manner and through her philosophy of care, reflected a transactional and transformational leadership style. Her tenacious courage, spirit of hospitality, and boundless enthusiasm kept order in the homes and ensured that tasks were accomplished in a timely manner. Relying on her deep faith, centered on Carmelite spirituality and inspired by God, she undertook a vision to care for the most vulnerable—the aged and infirm. Her leadership reflected a philosophy of service over her own self-interest.

She had a great desire to encourage others through her own actions and to foster in her sisters an investment of energy and commitment in things that really matter. She passed onto the sisters and, in turn, onto their lay leaders, a unique calling of living out the mission and core values of the Carmelite Sisters. As leaders in various positions of power and influence espouse this healing ministry that has been entrusted to them, they strive to make it visible and known to others. Through their actions, they hold this gift of stewardship as a sacred trust.

STAYING BALANCED THROUGH REFLECTION

Today, Catholic long-term care facilities are assuming greater numbers of frail elderly due to the influx of more senior citizens needing care than ever before. In this burgeoning system of care, emerging leaders must find an integrated balance of body, mind, and spirit. Occasionally, we experience work taking over and consuming our very existence. Work that once rewarded us now begins to drain us of our energy, joy, and commitment. It can begin in a subtle manner—until we look back and realize that we were so busy doing what leaders do that we were not being what ministry leaders are called to be.

The difference comes in maintaining a reflective way of life, a life that must continually nourish the inner spirit and provide a mission-driven, values-based compass that can navigate the rustling waters of organizational life time and time again and still remain safe.

Learning how to lead through the inspiration of Judeo-Christian values is at the spiritual core of ministry leadership. Leaders need to rely upon both their head and heart when engaging in ministry. This requires leaders to be driven by a set of values that reach across personal, community, and organizational aspects of their lives.

THE NEED FOR LAY LEADERSHIP FORMATION

Catholic long-term care in the United States is a highly-regulated industry with national, state, and organizational compliance standards. Nursing home leaders have demonstrated their technical competence by maintaining order to keep the organization going forward, ensuring that assignments are completed in a timely manner and ensuring that quality compliance standards are met for ongoing state accreditation. It is in this environment that ministry formation is essential to ensure continued leadership competency into the future. It is critical to address the unmet need for leadership formation and development for upcoming leaders in Catholic long-term care and other mission-driven organizations.

In 2004, the Catholic Health Association of the United States (CHA) conducted a study, the summary findings of which were published in a *Health Progress* article titled "What is Leadership Formation Now?" The article addressed the fact that the future of Catholic health care ministries depends upon leaders who answer the call to service in their communities, utilizing their personal gifts to galvanize those they lead to serve in a manner that reflects the mission and values of Catholic health care.

Indeed, there has been a transition from religious leadership to lay leadership that has emerged over the past several decades. Lay formation is essential if future leaders are to be influenced by and grounded in the mission and values of the heritage they are assuming.

TERESA'S WISDOM FOR HEALTH CARE LEADERS

Teresa of Avila reminds us that in doing ministry, we are the hands and feet of Christ in the workplace and society. Development of future leaders Catholic health care and other mission-driven organizations will serve as a key element in continuing this rich and viable ministry of the Church in the face of complex social, financial, and ethical issues both now and in the years to come.

Christ has no body on earth but yours, no hands but yours, no feet but yours. Yours are the eyes though which Christ's compassion for the world is to look out; yours are the feet with which He is to go about doing good; and yours are the hands with which He is to bless us now.
Saint Teresa of Avila

TURNING A PAGE: A NEW CHAPTER FOR LEADERS

Until very recently, Catholic long-term care ministries offered periodic or no formal ministry development to its lay leaders. The health care industry in the United States is changing at record speeds and challenges Catholic health care, particularly long-term care, in its attempts to provide compassionate care to an aging and frail population with fewer financial and human resources. Long-term care organizations would be the recipients of the least amount of reimbursement for services provided to the elderly under the American Health Care Act proposed in 2017, as opposed to previously, when Medicare or Medicaid received more funding in the before and during the Affordable Care Act era.

The elderly in the United States sign up and pay for Medicare as their primary health insurance, and as they grow older and frailer, they often move to a long-term care facility, where they draw down on their own life savings to offset the payment by

Medicare to the facility. When their funds have been depleted, they can apply for Medicaid, which will reimburse the facility about half of the actual cost of care for a resident. Catholic long-term care organizations accept Medicaid reimbursement, while numerous private and for-profit nursing homes do not. Maintaining quality of care for the aged and infirm is a priority for these Catholic facilities, and working to balance financial needs is paramount to ensure their effectiveness in the delivery of this care and an enhanced quality of life for residents.

It is in this context that emerging leaders must be formed to ensure the mission and values of the Catholic health care ministry continue to be the foundation upon which our elders are cared for. Lay ministry formation is essential to ensure the continued presence of the Church it its mission. Studying Judeo-Christian values, principles, and perspectives strengthens leaders' understanding of and commitment to these concepts. By embedding these values, principles, and perspectives within organizational operations, leaders are reflecting the grace of God in their work.

Acute-care systems have established formation programs for leadership, which have included education on topics such as the Catholic moral tradition and ethical decision-making, foundations of Catholic health care, values integration into operations, and principles of ministry leadership. More recently, elements of theological reflection have been added as a resource for discernment in leadership roles. (Though there are numerous methods in approaching theological reflection, for the purposes of this book, we will be focusing on the method of reflective thinking as an essential skillset for leaders.) The quick pace of activity in health care mandates that leaders oftentimes function in a multitasking environment in which they need to address multiple situations in a simultaneous manner. This multitasking behavior, if not addressed, can frequently lead to symptoms of distress or negative stress that drain energy and enhance burnout, including chronic fatigue, heightened anxiety, loss of appetite, forgetfulness, and moodiness. It can become exasperating for leaders in ministry settings, where the responsibility for successful resident care outcomes is placed squarely on their shoulders.

Leaders need to recognize when they are feeling stress, especially negative stress, as it can limit the leader's ability to perform at his or her highest level. Left unresolved, negative stress can have catastrophic consequences on the leader's mental and physical well-being. Figure 1 provides some signals indicating negative and positive stress.

Signals of Negative Stress	Signals of Positive Stress
Physical • Tense muscles, headaches • Change in eating and sleeping habits • Illness, ulcers, other health issues	*Physical* • Feeling fit and alert • Eating well • Good muscle tone
Emotional • Irritable • Distracted • Withdrawn	*Emotional* • Joyful • Focused • Confident, involved in activities
Spiritual • Sense of emptiness • Aversion to routine prayer/reflection • Hopeless, despairing attitude	*Spiritual* • Sense of purpose/meaning • Reflective, prayerful • Hopeful and trust in God
Behaviors • Sluggish • Manic—feeling "all over the place" • Inordinate use of drugs, alcohol, etc.	*Behaviors* • Energized • Balanced lifestyle • Striving to accomplish goals

Figure 1. Signals of Positive and Negative Stress

While such an environment within acute-care organizations is based upon quick patient turnover, this mentality can spill over into long-term care organizations as hospital discharges are rapidly referred to long-term care facilities by multiple providers. The resident environment in a Carmelite long-term care facility emphasizes a homelike atmosphere, which is supported by the incorporation of mission and values into daily life of the organization, while addressing the aforementioned challenges. Seeking a balance is the key for leaders, and their formative experiences in reflective thinking can assist in managing their stress.

PLANTING THE SEEDS OF ROOTS OF CARING

In 2011, The Catholic Health Association of the United States (CHA) published its *Framework for Senior Leadership Formation.* Various leadership topics, such as ethical decision-making, systems thinking, and workplace spirituality were outlined. Those topics were in the framework, along with sample suggestions that were provided from Catholic health systems, which had previously undertaken such initiatives, including theological reflection and the process of discernment. The goal of the document was to provide a resource that would contribute to more effective formation among leaders in Catholic health care.

Further work was undertaken in 2013 when CHA commissioned the Center for Applied Research in the Apostolate (CARA) to assess the effectiveness of ministry formation programs. Respondents reported that most of the formation programs they attended extended over a year or more, and each session lasted multiple days. Those who attended shorter programs stated that they felt learning about spirituality and theological reflection were essential components of their formation experience.

ROOTS OF CARING: MINISTRY LEADERSHIP

In 2012, referencing the aforementioned framework, the Carmelite Sisters initiated the Roots of Caring program to address the previously identified issues. The program was designed to fit with long-term care ministry and presented in three two-and-a-half-day sessions over an extended period of time. (The schedule was designed this way to accommodate the group of leaders in an effort to not keep them away for too long from the facilities at which they were employed; however, the teaching of reflective leadership does not demand this exact schedule, so it can be adapted to fit your needs.) Periodic readings were assigned between in-person sessions, and group conference calls were employed to discuss insights and share ideas that emerged from the readings.

Some topics presented during the in-person sessions included the "Carmelite Sisters' History and Heritage," "Mission and Values Integration," "*Ethical and Religious Directives for Catholic Health Care*," "Corporate Culture," "Cultural Diversity," "Catholic Social Teaching," and "Judeo-Christian Stories." Later, following the 2016 intensive, "Emotional and Spiritual Intelligence," and "Skills in Reflective Leadership" were added. These and other ministry-related themes were used during the presentations and discussion with participants.

In reviewing the Roots of Caring 1st and 2nd cohort graduates' evaluation summaries, the following comments were found: participants needed more time to process issues and desired to acquire further skills that could help manage stress reduction and help to improve their decision-making techniques. They indicated that working in a highly charged environment took its toll on them, and in continuing formation sessions, they wanted time to ponder, absorb, and integrate what had been presented.

REFLECTIVE LEADERSHIP: GOING FURTHER

These statements contributed to a realization that Roots of Caring, while excellent, was not providing exposure to a process of reflective leadership. Therefore, those who participated in ongoing formation would be exposed to a concentrated process to foster opportunities for deeper personal introspection and expanded leadership potential. This process would potentially enhance their self-directed coping methods toward stress reduction and efficient decision-making abilities, while increasing their commitment to reflective ministry leadership.

Since Roots of Caring already possessed an established and well-seasoned curriculum, it was decided by the Carmelite Sisters to offer continuing formation for graduates of the program. The Sisters support the premise that it is from these graduates that future administrators and assistant administrators of the ministry could be selected. Participants are aware of this fact and continue to participate as an opportunity for them to expand their leadership knowledge and be part of an experience that could enhance their careers in Catholic long-term care.

THE BEGINNING OF THE PROCESS

In both October 2016 and prior to participating in the continuing formation program, each participant was asked to complete a fifteen-question, five-point value scale pre-program survey. This survey was constructed from values-based materials specific to the Carmelite Sisters long-term care ministries. Its language is understood by those who minister and is reflective of the cultural climate in which they are committed to the aged and infirm.

Question subset 1–5 identified a combined pre-program survey score of 4.1% and was directed toward *community dimensions* for leaders to extend, manifest, demonstrate or encourage supportive behavior by their actions.

The combined pre-program survey results indicated that question subset 6–10 ranked highest with 4.2% and focused on *organizational dimensions* for leaders to look at, consider, support and act upon in their life and work.

The final and lowest score for question subset 11–15 was 3.9% and focused on *personal dimensions*, asking respondents to be mindful, understanding, encouraging and reflective.

These pre-program survey results were instrumental in designing the content for the continuing education formation intensive seminar. The results led to topics being identified that were applicable to a leaders' inner growth and development, the organizational challenges they face and the community interactions necessary to be successful in the ministry. Results from the post-program survey are presented in Chapter Six.

	Topic of Discussion/Response	Average Score
1)	I extend hospitality to all those I encounter in my ministry.	4.3
2)	I demonstrate the dignity of persons in my actions as a leader.	4.2
3)	I manifest the Mission of the Organization in my daily work.	4.2
4)	I encourage a spirit of compassion in the workplace.	3.8
5)	I act on behalf of justice issues for staff, residents and family members.	3.9
6)	I look to our organizational values as a guide in my decision making.	4.2
7)	I consider how God is present in our facility.	4.1
8)	I act to alleviate discrimination of the aged and vulnerable elderly.	4.1
9)	I believe that caring for the elderly is a way to reduce human suffering.	4.4
10)	I support attending to the needs of the whole person; body, mind and spirit.	4.2
11)	I am mindful of organizational resources and use them wisely.	4.0
12)	I understand the experience of suffering as being wider than sickness.	4.1
13)	I reflect on the human condition of others when considering the common good.	3.7
14)	I engage in a thoughtful process when making integral decisions.	3.8
15)	I consider my work a Christian witness to those I serve in word and deed.	4.1

Figure 2. Roots of Caring Pre-Program Survey Results

MY PONDERING

I came to realize this project was a form of personal calling for me. I found myself being drawn inward to reflect upon my years of ministry leadership in Catholic health care and the people who touched my life along that journey. Many staff and leaders demonstrated time and again the commitment and call they had to serving those in great need. Their recognition of their work as ministry, no matter their own faith traditions, served as inspiration for me to continue in my leadership role.

I have come to believe from my own faith experience, personal reflection and Christian values that my behavior and actions are influenced by my own call to ministry, which grounds me and provides me with identity, purpose and meaning in life. We only come to this by taking time in our lives to pause, pray, think about and reflect upon our individual purpose (i.e., mission) in life and the stepping stones (i.e., values) that provide us with the directions we need to maintain a moral compass. Mission and values become more formidable when incorporated into the reflective process that leaders use when they make decisions that impact those they serve.

QUESTIONS FOR REFLECTION

1. Where are the opportunities for you to grow in leadership?

2. How do you live in the present while juggling issues of the past and future?

3. What provides you a sense of balance in your life and work to reduce stressors?

NOTES

2

WISDOM LEADESHIP: INSIGHTS FROM STRUGGLE AND SUFFERING

"The feeling remains that God is on the journey too."
St. Teresa of Avila

Leaders from past and present centuries hold one thing in common: they have suffered. Their suffering may have been a result of physical, emotional, or spiritual trauma they have gone through while being leader, or it may have been the trauma experienced by a loved one that contributed to their suffering. In either case, the unspoken and unacknowledged stressors that exist within us usually take their toll. Every decision has consequences, good or bad, over the course of time. Those in leadership are all too often placed in a quandary of being a leader for all while not revealing the vulnerable, isolated, or lonely side of themselves. This, too, contributes toward their suffering.

THE JOURNEYS OF MOSES AND PAUL
The Judeo-Christian tradition is one source from which suffering was part and parcel of its beginning. In reading and reflecting upon passages or stories from both the Old and New Testament, you will find stalwart individuals who, through transformative experiences, embrace their roles as leaders. In the Old Testament, Moses is called to leadership from his encounter with a burning bush, but he is resistant to accept this role because of his own sense of inadequacy—though God seemed to know better! He is told by God that he is on holy ground, to remove his sandals, and come closer to the bush. He does so. He listens. He may not fully understand, but he accepts

his commission and will lead his people out of slavery.

He becomes a champion for the Jewish people, who find freedom in Moses' leadership and follow him into the desert with the anticipated hope of returning to the promised land. He successfully leads them home, and, while having experienced numerous struggles and disappointments along the journey, Moses' leadership stands firm in his mission.

In the New Testament, Saul, who once persecuted Christians, has an experience on the road to Damascus in being thrown from his horse and hearing the words "Why do you persecute me?" In this profound experience, Saul, the aggressor of those who are Christian, is transformed into Paul, the evangelizer of Christianity to the Gentile communities.

STRUGGLE: THE WISDOM OF MOSES AND PAUL

If we pause and reflect on these two stories and the experiences that Moses and Paul went through in their time and place, we can take from them meaning and purpose to apply to our lives today. In the details of their lives, you will find what they hold in common is the encounter with the divine that they listened to, a willingness to grapple with what they heard, an attempt to understand their call, and the taking upon themselves the mantle of leadership in sharing their vision. Through their journeys, they encountered struggle, doubt, challenges, and loss of faith in their leadership. In between the lines of these stories is the pearl of wisdom in becoming a suffering leader who works through the experience and emerges stronger, wiser, and humbler in their realization of the call to be an instrument of God by fulfilling their mission.

Becoming aware that struggle and suffering is a learning experience in life is a resource from which we can deepen our faith and grow closer to and become conscious of God's work in and through us. As leaders, we do not intentionally desire to struggle or suffer, but it is a reality that all of us face from time to time. Our inner self struggles to grasp the stark reality of a dramatic encounter with a decision we're facing or when we suffer from being impacted by an organizational action that was necessary, yet painful for ourselves and others.

Unchecked struggle and suffering can become a pattern in our leadership style and ultimately start to weaken our ability to lead effectively. A key in responding to these challenges is to identify our inner strengths. We must develop our ability to be resilient in the face of adversity by reflecting upon the situation before us and our response to it, no matter how difficult. In doing so, we can, over the course of time, grow wiser and more insightful.

A VISIONARY LEADER BEFORE HER TIME

St. Teresa of Avila's writings bring significant insight to the life of prayer and her own experience of suffering. She lived in the 16th century (1515–1582) and was the daughter of a wealthy Spanish merchant. Her mother died when she was young, and her personal struggles as a teenager brought her father to send her to a boarding convent. Teresa stayed there for several years and returned home with the intention of not marrying, but rather of becoming a Carmelite nun at the age of twenty. Her initial experience in the Carmelites was positive during her formative years; however, as time went by, she grew lax in her prayer life and found the convent to be an environment of spiritual mediocrity. She frequently refers to the convent as more of a boarding house than a place of prayer due to the great number of sisters in the same community convent.

A dramatic shift took place within her at the age of thirty-nine: Teresa had a profound conversion experience and found herself drawn to establishing a new religious community of Carmelites, who lived a simple life in small numbers (never to be greater than twelve). They became known as the "Discalced" or "Shoeless" Carmelites and lived a quiet, interior life focused on prayer and meditating on the passion of Christ and the life of the Holy Family. Teresa found that, as cloistered nuns, she and others exerted significant influence. She not only led a reform movement for her new community, which grew rapidly in number, but also drew upon her natural-born administrative skills so as to found other convents throughout Spain—twelve in total prior to her death.

TERESA'S *INTERIOR CASTLE*

In the *Interior Castle,* Teresa describes seven stages or levels of prayer than can be attained through the process of individual spiritual development. While she wrote the *Interior Castle* for her Sisters, her unique vision, personal insight, and administrative shrewdness contribute greatly to appreciating her life circumstances and the era in which she lived. One interpretation of her writings surfaces through the lens of human and spiritual development in our present day. The imagery Teresa used in the *Interior Castle* was rooted in the spiritual theology of her era. Teresa viewed the castle as a metaphor for the soul (individual); the castle has an abundance of rooms, each with its own identity, that the individual can enter and leave as desired. Throughout the text, she also employs various archetypes of romance and imagery of fountains and silkworms to provide the reader with visual analogies that align a persons' prayer life and spiritual growth. In this chapter, we will explore the journey through the Castles' and discuss their significance to leadership today.

Teresa wrote that the door to the inner castle, and therefore to true self-knowledge, was prayer and reflection. She viewed prayer as an intimate sharing between friends; however, her assumption is that our friend—God—is the one who first speaks. The mystery at the center of the castle first "spoke" us into our lives, into wider freedom and more intimate union. We are essentially listeners for this voice, hearers of the word. Prayer, therefore, requires attentiveness.

THE KEY TO WISDOM: REFLECTION ON EXPERIENCE

In Teresa's writings, the word *experience* is the opposite of *theory*. Experience is to know something by having lived, felt, or gone through it. It is from common, multiple life experiences—lights and shadows, victories and defeats, successes and disappointments, a good direction or losing one's way—that we are transformed. Woven through Teresa's thoughts is her insightfulness and sense of the presence of God in her midst (listening), her having an open mind and spirit to interpret that presence (understanding) and an inner strength or fiber to communicate her experiences (sharing) in writing. These traits are present-day components of reflective leadership.

Teresa found the motto from Proverbs "that He found his delight in the children of men" to be an inspirational source for her writings. Teresa understood the truth of Proverbs to be the unique, Holy relationship between God and humans. It is this quote that reveals God's love for His creation.

As an introduction to the *Interior Castle*, Teresa writes that she is following orders from her superiors to write so that the sisters in the convent may have their questions about prayer answered. The year was 1577, and she was in the Carmelite monastery in Toledo, Spain.

It is during the time of the Spanish Inquisition, and she is keenly aware that the eyes of the Church are upon her. In fact, her book on her life was sequestered by the Inquisition and published only after her death. As she writes the format of each of the castles, she weaves into her prose the themes of listening to God through the Sacred Scriptures, being intentional toward daily meditation as a source of understanding, and deepening your relationship with God. She realized that her inspired written words were her primary source of sharing these philosophies with others. In her writings, Teresa becomes the true storyteller of the Carmelite contemplative life.

INSIGHTS FROM TERESA'S FIRST THREE CASTLES

The first three Castles are the arena in which we begin to develop our identity and the unique elements of our character that comprise our individuality. They allow us to draw from them the insight that leaders need to use self-knowledge and reflection to identify our *vision*, explore our inner call to discern our *mission*, and encounter and sift through struggles, challenges, delays, and other sufferings to arrive at a well-ordered life that emerges by being grounded in our *values*.

In the First Castle, Teresa invites the individual (soul) to be aware of self-knowledge through prayer, reflection, and the consciousness of God's presence and the soul's beauty. In the Second Castle, Teresa implores us to pursue an inner call to retrieve our identity or true purpose in life. In the Third Castle, Teresa identifies life's obstacles that must be overcome, such as separation, loneliness, humiliation and pain, in order to grow closer to the one you love. In her case, she is referring to God and her own willingness to encounter suffering, endurance, and patience, each of which are a challenge in her life.

A PERSONAL TRANSFORMATION

In my own life, I was what might be considered a "Type A" personality. All that was overshadowed when I had an emergency triple bypass procedure. I previously had stents placed into my arteries, but the stents collapsed, and the result prior to the bypass was my momentarily dying on the table and being brought back through God's will and medical technology. The bypass saved my life, and during this "in-between" experience, I saw the great comforting white light. It was an out-of-body experience for me, and I believe it was a once in a lifetime afterlife encounter with the Divine Being of God. It did, as Teresa suggests, bring with it a plethora of health-related issues. However, I have come to my realization that God is not done with me yet. I find that, as time has passed, I have learned to reintroduce myself to the person in my body. It works differently for eating and digesting, for energy and limitations, for retention and recall. In these and other aspects of my life, I have become both thankful and humbled to still be alive for myself, my family, and my friends.

I live each day in the belief of being on borrowed time, and I am grateful to God for permitting me to continue to share and learn from those I love. I find myself seeing God present in small ways, such as the kindness of others toward me or the laughter of my wife, daughter, son-in-law, granddaughter, and grandson. I find joy in staying connected with close friends. My ministry as both a deacon and an educator has been rewarding for me, and I have been privileged to see God working in and through those I have been called to serve. I'm aware that my prayer life has grown deeper each day since the bypass. I engage in morning and evening prayer and in Lectio Divina by reflecting on the scripture of the day. I participate in a small prayer group where I find the richness of our readings and discussions to be nourishing, insightful, and a source of reflection.

QUIET TIME TO RENEW YOUR INNER SPIRIT

During the initial writing of the *Interior Castle*, Teresa suffered from an internal crisis that led her to come to grips with psychophysical exhaustion. She took time off from writing, remained in seclusion, read up on herbal treatments, and ate various herbs and soups to alleviate the headaches and exhaustion. Once she rested and regained her strength, Teresa once again threw herself into her prayer life, her work, and her writing as a means of managing her depression while simultaneously sharing her experiences of listening to and understanding God's presence in our lives. Teresa is very familiar with the mystery of human suffering, since poor health followed her for over forty years.

EXPLORING TERESA'S FOURTH CASTLE

In the Fourth Castle, the soul is granted the gift of quiet. I find that quiet from interior prayer serves me well each day. The morning time especially serves as source of inspiration, prayerful insight, and thankfulness. This centering continues to deepen my prayer and well-being in life, and I have found that it's not a repetitive experience, but rather a time for daily renewal of my spirit. Becoming conscious of the fact that you are a morning or evening person and what time your inner energy emerges best is an important part of being an effective leader.

In this Fourth Castle, Teresa employs the imagery of two fountains. The first image is of water that is drawn from far away and with much effort, in much the same way as we meditate. The second image places the water as a fountain that flows continuously.

In his youth, Pope John Paul II was influenced by a tailor named Jan Tyranowski, who had a mystical bent and introduced him to the practice of the Carmelite way of spirituality. Pope John Paul II was able perceive that Teresa's writings were applicable to the world in which he lived, particularly with respect to the struggles of faith that experienced by generations of the late-twentieth and early twenty-first centuries. He recognized that Teresa was able to communicate the human experience how prayer and reflection helped one to better understand God's goodness and His mercy.

Pope John Paul II's theology of suffering as stated in *On the Christian Meaning of Human Suffering* manifests itself from deep spiritual roots within him that were fostered when he was young by listening to mentors who formed him and to the voice of God. Just like Teresa's imagery of the fountain that flowed freely from the spring, so too his depth of prayer, reflection, and inspiration have come forth from understanding life's struggles, sorrows, and personal suffering to refresh and renew our spirit in time of need by sharing his words of wisdom.

TERESA'S FIFTH, SIXTH, AND SEVENTH CASTLES

Continuing on in the Fifth Mansion, Teresa likens the experience of coming out of prayer to the transformative process of change that a silkworm undergoes as it's emerging from its cocoon as a white butterfly. The Sixth Castle is where the soul is tried, but it is also where the soul begins to understand something about its future, strengthening one's resolve to suffer the struggles of life. In the Seventh Castle the soul is invited to unify with God—the ultimate reward for navigating adversity and suffering. In these writings, we find the experience of the soul, our consciousness, being given the opportunity to experience the inner light in addition to the external light.

Suffering can be like a grain of sand in an oyster. It can irritate and annoy us by continuing to rub us the wrong way; it becomes a constant in our lives, but over time, it can emerge into a pearl that is bright and shiny. When that occurs, it's as if we forget about the previous pain and focus on the beauty that has emerged from the experience.

In learning from our and others' struggles and suffering, ministry leaders can bring forth keen insight when responding to the call to leadership. It is in the quiet, inner depth of personal reflection and discernment that we encounter the holy, the experience of the presence of God in our midst. This is the time to pause and be open to the inner voice calling us, drawing us forward to face the encounters that await us. These encounters can provide us with an energy inspired by faith in God, a hope driven in what we are undertaking and an increased love for what we do and whom we serve as leaders.

OPENNESS TO LEARN: A READINESS FOR LEADERS

Teresa is eloquent in the way she comes to experience, understand, and share her leadership challenges and personal sufferings. In the *Interior Castle*, Teresa sees the first three mansions as the strong foundation from which a soul is able to enter into the remaining ones, and I find that the older I become, the more I am able to surrender my control over to God. It is an ongoing struggle for me, but I have experienced the joy that comes with trying to listen more clearly, seeking to understand what I hear more readily, and being open enough to share my insights with others more freely.

QUESTIONS FOR REFLECTION

1. Are you aware of suffering in your own life? How have you accepted or fought it?

2. Has suffering deepened your understanding of God's place in your life?

3. Are you able to empathize with others because of your own suffering? Give some examples of this from your ministry.

NOTES

_____

_____

_____

_____

_____

_____

_____

_____

_____

_____

_____

_____

_____

_____

_____

_____

_____

_____

_____

_____

3

LEARNING FROM LEADERS WHO CAME BEFORE US

"...And the Blind Man said 'one thing I do know
is that I was blind and now I see'"
John 9:25

WISDOM OF LEADERS FROM THE DISTANT PAST

There have been times in my life when I have been profoundly influenced by a leader who possessed both dignity or the ability to self-examine issues in detail and the ease in which the leader effectively communicates with those they are encountering.

Francis of Assisi

Francis of Assisi (1182–1226) was the son of a successful Italian merchant and loving mother. In growing up, he turned from being a troubadour to become a soldier who was wounded in a battle and later imprisoned for a year prior to release. His freedom initially led him to a life of wandering until the time that he was able to listen attentively to God's call to serve the poor and needy of Assisi, Italy. His vision spread and, in time, grew to over ten thousand brothers across the continent. Francis is renowned for his engagement with the environment and all its creatures as well as his *Canticle of Creatures* describing earthly goods that give sustenance to us and glory to God.

Ignatius of Loyola

Ignatius of Loyola (1491–1556) came from a family of nobility in the Basque region of the northern part of Spain. He was initially vain and held dreams of fame and honor for his actions. At the age of thirty, Ignatius found himself as an officer in the Spanish army. In an intense battle among the French troops, he was struck in the leg with a cannonball and brought back for surgery, recovery, and care. He asked for reading material that spoke of chivalry and was given the only books available, which were about the lives of the saints. Ignatius read these with passion and found the stories riveting, especially the one on Francis of Assisi, possibly due to similar battle circumstances in their lives. As Ignatius continued getting better, he felt an inner voice prompting him to pursue a vison of service to those unschooled and in need of education.

Later, upon his full recovery Ignatius went to Paris, where he found several companions with whom he shared his vision. Together, they became the first Jesuits, and Ignatius compiled the Spiritual Exercises as a source for him and his followers to rely upon each day in their prayers and discernment.

My Reflections on Past Wisdom Leaders

Francis of Assisi and Ignatius of Loyola, along with Teresa of Avila, have become sources of inspiration for me, not only for what they faced in their time and place, but also for how they faced it—relying upon God and their ability to pause, reflect, and learn. In their experience of struggle and suffering, they leave us with a legacy of wisdom for leadership today.

HEALTH CARE: THE "ESSENTIAL MINISTRY"

One such individual who learned from his experience of struggle and suffering was the late Cardinal Joseph Bernardin. Following his diagnosis of pancreatic cancer, he chose to share his journey and experience of suffering. He wrote about the suffering of Jesus, which far exceeded the depths we may know, and how Jesus' ability to let himself suffer in the pursuit of something greater than himself brought wisdom. In a 1988 talk he gave to the American College of Health Care Administrators, he stressed the importance of leaders of Catholic health care caring for and supporting one another through life.

Bernardin viewed health care as critical to the mission of the Catholic Church because it was especially capable of providing hope so badly needed by the ill. He urged Catholic institutions to collaborate in order to survive competitive financial pressures and hark back to their religious mission of providing hope, comfort, and a sense that the sick and elderly are part of a community.

THE CARMELITE SISTERS' MINISTRY

The ministry of Catholic long-term care is distinct in its purpose, which is devoted to service of the elderly. This purpose is affirmed through ministries of the Carmelite Sisters for the Aged and Infirm, who are guided by the seven-point philosophy of Mother Angeline. The work engaged in through this ministry brings present and emerging leaders along with support staff up close and into the daily lives of the elderly. Those who partake in Catholic health care organizations as staff, patients, or residents can experience quality, compassionate care.

In times of sickness, frailty, and loss of independence, we tend to bunker down to protect the remaining threads of our vulnerable self. Mother Angeline knew this when she founded this Community. She, like Teresa of Avila, faced challenges, joys, and sorrows. Through her sustaining vision, reflective prayer life, and selfless commitment to others, Mother Angeline succeeded in bringing the elderly a life filled with hospitality and compassion while exemplifying sanctity of life for all and a shared commitment to the service of the aged and infirm in the United States. Both of these women experienced suffering throughout their lives.

Down through the centuries and generations, it has been seen that in suffering there is concealed a particular power that draws a person closer to God, a life-changing experience that enables us to hear with new ears and see with new eyes. Mother Angeline was frequently known to say, "I think the best of all prayer is just to kneel or sit quietly and let Jesus pour Himself into our souls."

Throughout her life, she practiced and encouraged others to reflect upon Sacred Scripture. In practicing reflective thinking, we come to observe that when we're reflective, we are inwardly listening. When we open our mind and heart to interpret the reflection, we begin to understand what meaning and message is being given to us. When we gently communicate our insight with others, we are sharing our wisdom.

"I think the best of all prayer is just to kneel or sit quietly and let Jesus pour Himself into our souls."
Mother Angeline Teresa McCrory, O. Carm.

RECOGNIZING SUFFERING TO BEGIN HEALING

Christians believe that the life and death of Jesus shows us how to live and die. The gospel calls us to take up our cross willingly and carry it, learn from it, understand its purpose in our lives, and share that journey with those we encounter. Jesus is the Christian model for living with suffering. Much of what patients and residents experience in Catholic acute and long-term care facilities is the brittleness of humanity made manifest in the presence of a loving God.

Suffering impacts not only the lives of those afflicted, but also family, friends, and staff who encounter them. It draws on their feelings and emotions and the realization of the fragileness of life in this world for us all. In many instances, family and friends do not visit their loved one frequently because it serves as a close reminder that we are vulnerable to sickness. By denying our own potential for illness, we can bury our feelings of empathy and sadness. Illness, especially chronic illness, has a tendency to exhibit in family members a symptom of low-grade depression as a means of protecting themselves.

Those who are the caregivers have the opportunity to witness the change in the one who is sick and observe the sense of peace that comes with their self-acceptance and reconciliation. Those engaged in the Carmelite ministries to the aged and infirm have come to know and experience the healing touch of God in those they serve.

FROM EXPERIENCE TO REFLECTION

Teresa of Avila reminds us that experience is something we feel, know, or have gone through and has the potential to transform our lives if we take time to reflect. We can encounter this through our own redemptive suffering and in recognizing for ourselves the spirituality of Teresa of Avila and the religious inspiration of Venerable Mother Angeline Teresa McCrory, O. Carm.

Chapters 2 and 3 have drawn from the experience and reflections of these leaders from the distant and recent past as a way of exposing present ministry leaders to finding personal insights from these wisdom figures. It is in our pausing to take time and reflect upon words such as these that we can hopefully strengthen our own conviction to the call of reflective leadership and service to others in need.

QUESTIONS FOR REFLECTION

1. How has the experience of profound change impacted your leadership style?

2. When have other leaders, past or present, been an inspiration to you? What did you learn?

3. How does the sense of the sacred get incorporated into your leadership?

NOTES

4

THE EXPERIENCE OF KNOWLEDGE TO INSIGHT

"Our mind is capable of passing beyond the
dividing line we have drawn for it."
Herman Hesse

As mentioned in the previous chapter, wisdom and reflection play off one another. Together, they can enlighten our minds and hearts and serve as sources of new energy and inspiration. As we reflect, there is a greater chance for awareness from listening to the voice of God emerging from within us. Reflection can be understood as stepping back from the mirror, getting a more in-depth perspective, then taking a moment to observe what is happening within ourselves. It allows us to see life patterns as lived through our values and place meaning on our actions. Pausing to look deep down within ourselves can bring each of us face-to-face with our most transparent self. I have found throughout my experiences, good and bad alike, that reflection provides an opportunity to become more conscious of the presence of God working in and through our lives.

The very act of taking time out of a busy, fast-paced life seems, on the surface, untenable. Our minds are bombarded with all types of stimulation vying for our mental attention in today's electronic world. It may appear that reflective methods, theologically based or not, are inconsequential to our daily responsibilities and actions. However, experience with reflection can tell you otherwise. Existentialist Soren Kierkegaard said that "life can only be understood backwards, but it must be lived forward." His insight from the past brings forth wisdom for our future. Living in the present, being conscious of life's bumps along the way, and working to have a clear vision for our future are all experiential aspects that can be readily applied to the art of reflection as we journey.

THE CASE FOR TEACHING REFLECTIVE LEADERSHIP

Reflection is a learned process that can bring about subtle, yet profound change in our very being if we are open to it. It is through reflection that we allow our experiences to process and create deeper meaning for ourselves. It is the mode through which we can best experience self-discovery and self-awareness. In her era, Teresa of Avila would have concurred with this sentiment, since it complements her understanding of experience. The process of practicing reflection permits us to look at important issues and realize that how we see the results could change as we filter them through increased knowledge.

A 2014 *Health Progress* article from the Ministry Leadership Center in Sacramento, California, indicated that ongoing ministry leadership development helps increase participants' awareness, which ultimately informs behaviors. Reflective leadership calls upon twenty-first century leaders to develop introspective and observant skills, as Teresa of Avila did, which allow for the growth of creative thinking, honesty, and integrity in becoming transformational leaders.

Summary results of a national survey commissioned in 2013 by the Catholic Health Association of the United States and conducted in 2014 by the Center for Applied Research in the Apostolate (CARA) on Catholic health care formation programs for lay leadership found that while programs differed in length of time and varied in content based upon the desire of the sponsor and needs of the participants, reflective thinking was commonly cited as an exercise that enhanced the leadership formation process.

In my opinion, based on over thirty years of engaging in ministry leadership formation, I observed Catholic health, social service, and pastoral leaders who participated in ministry formation programs that have employed a reflective method find the process enables them to step back and gain perspective on their actions and decisions that have had an impact on their own lives and the lives of others. I have come to believe that it is in the very act of using a reflective method that the potential for expanded insight and informed wisdom can emerge and thereby transform present and future leaders into more effective ministry leaders.

Over the course of my career, I was enriched by colleagues from across the United States. I found that in coming together, we often scheduled time for prayer and liturgy. The experience of being with and listening to one another frequently provided the larger context of meaning for me to more deeply value the day-in, day-out work of health care. Together, we came to understand and share the fact that our inner spirituality manifests itself in our actions that are values-based and congruent with the mission of the organization and the lay leaders who see their role as a call, thereby recognizing that ministerial leadership has evolved as an outgrowth of ministry formation.

PROGRAM DEVELOPMENT FOR ADULT LEARNERS

In creating program content for leaders, it was essential for me to understand at the outset their needs as learners, as well as what should be taken into consideration when developing the program format and the resources utilized. Relying upon my knowledge of education, my prior experience from program evaluation summaries, and my experience teaching and presenting to adults, I have found that adult learners, for the most part, are visual and/or auditory learners. That is to say, they would rather read an article than have it read to them as a means of retention.

Visual learners have a propensity to think in pictures and vivid mental images, learning more easily and recalling ideas and concepts better if they are illustrated on a white board, PowerPoint, or handout. They oftentimes see the big picture of an issue before others do, are proficient public speakers, and are, more often than not, competent, effective leaders. They frequently learn by seeing or hearing new information being presented, observing and participating in role play situations, engaging in case studies appropriate to their work environment, and discussing the relevant application of the content materials presented. Each of these methods offers salient teaching and learning techniques that adults have found beneficial to their personal and professional growth and development.

Employing these methods and having participants work on

a series of case studies while using a reflective method enabled them to identify with real situations from their own work experience. They were instructed to reflect upon the case studies as a group and respond to the issues presented by analyzing, critiquing, and expressing their opinion of the overall case presentation; this provided a forum of "learning by doing." In their interaction with each case, they identified the desire to begin with an *experience* they encountered and were able to reconstruct retrospectively by listening to the voice within guide them. This was followed by the ability to *reflect* on their involvement with the case from various personal, psychosocial, and scriptural-based references that enhanced their understanding of the event. Finally, they could *respond*, having gained further knowledge by their sharing with peers in a safe place of the entire experience.

THE JOHARI WINDOW

The concept of reflective leadership is oftentimes traced back to a 1955 behavioral model for leadership called the Johari Window, named for its creators, Joe Luft and Harry Ingham. It is composed of four quadrants, which represent our lives: the *arena*, where we see ourselves and others see us; the *blind spot* that we don't see, but others do; the *façade* as a segment of my life that I know but choose not to reveal to others; and the *unknown*, an aspect of myself that is in the process of emerging and evolving, of which I lack awareness at the present time. This model is fluid and changes as we grow, develop, and are willing to be self-revealing. This lifelong process is not easy and should not be taken lightly. To become a reflective leader is a vocation to search within oneself, to adjust our lens of vision and draw on a desire to see our experiences in a new light.

Though the Johari Window appears to be simple concept to grasp, I found it to be a core ingredient for this project. It illustrates what we and others know or do not know about us. It can serve as a foundational reference point for those being introduced to reflective leadership. Stages of reflective leadership are similar to teaching someone to swim. You enter the shallow water and become more acquainted and at ease with it, just like becoming comfortable with what you see and know about yourself in the Johari Window. You learn basic swimming strokes and see your skills develop before your very eyes before gaining confidence to enter into the deep waters.

It also models for us a way of explaining the process of self-revelation within reflection. It shows us the possibility of going into the unknown area of our lives. The process of reflection can be viewed as a life preserver to rely upon when we need to navigate rough waters in our decision-making. Like the life preserver, reflection methods keep us afloat and permit us to be part of the water, but not submerged under it, similar to using reflective resources to keep our view from being obstructed while we discern how to proceed. It allows us to present our authentic selves in a way that motivates and influences others.

In a formative process for ministry leaders, it is essential to address the overall aspects of the Johari Window as a framework to explore oneself by being quiet and taking the time to go within and journey down into our inner self. Those who participate in ongoing ministry leadership are often persons who are seekers. They are willing to be open to new learning and growth opportunities and, at times, experience murky breakthroughs and challenging insights for themselves and those they are called to lead.

GUIDING LEADERSHIP STYLE

Retrospectively, I have come to realize that our beliefs are taught and passed onto us when we are children. Attitudes are instilled in us as young adults by what we observe and participate in within our family system and among our peers. When we emerge as adults, our values have been honed, so we can venture into our world of work and encounter issues in applying our experiential learning. Oftentimes, ministry leaders in all venues learn from their experiences, seek out mentors who can guide them along the way, and profit from the hands-on, experience-based knowledge that comes with reflecting on their lives and work. Such individuals demonstrate an emerging transformational leadership style that serves as an expression of ministerial leadership.

In recent times, Catholic health care leaders have found their need to develop transformational skills and styles in order to succeed into the future health care delivery system. Transformational leadership requires leaders to make good decisions for all concerned parties, which is accomplished through the use of developed listening skills, an inquisitive nature, and an openness to diverse perspectives and solutions. Wisdom is the product of leaders' reflection on their actions. This is in contrast to transactional leaders, who maintain the status quo, do not rock the boat, and ensure that the organization's culture remains intact. Transactional leaders emphasize corrective action and rewards only when performance expectations are met by others.

TRANSFORMING THROUGH REFLECTION

As we move forward, these two styles must be enhanced by reflective leadership. The time has come to ensure that both the head and the heart of the matter are working together for the good of the ministry. Transforming leaders must incorporate their reflective skills of intellectual, emotional, and spiritual insight into being fully present to those they are called to serve. Through deep thinking and empathy, leaders can motivate others, communicate vision, and embody the mission.

Ministry leaders who embody transformational leadership traits will achieve the most success in their personal call and experience positive outcomes by leading through their presence. Their organization can become a more emotionally healthy, mission-driven, and values-based place to work.

PROVIDING HOPE THROUGH PRESENCE

In Catholic health care ministry, *presence* is understood as the ability to provide a source of hope by accompanying another person who is in some form of distress or disease. This occurs one-on-one in medical centers, hospitals, and long-term care facilities throughout the country. But disease and distress can also appear in the life of the organization in ways that exhibit dysfunction, namely when mission and values are not central to the operations and consistent decision-making of the facility. Such a reality demonstrates the shadow side of organizational life. Moving from the dark side into the light necessitates leadership that is ministry-centered, focusing on the good of the whole instead of personal achievements only.

The Gospel of Matthew states, "as you go, make this proclamation: The kingdom of heaven is at hand. Cure the sick, raise the dead, cleanse lepers, drive out demons. Without cost you have received; without cost you are to give." This gospel reflects the journey that the early disciples undertook, and down through the ages to the present time, we understand that when embarking on a journey each of us needs nourishment along the way. Ministry leaders can find that source of sustenance in the work they undertake, in the inspiration of coworkers, in the appreciation of those they provide educational, pastoral, or social services to (as well as oversight and care for patients and residents in Catholic hospitals and long-term care facilities), and in their ability to deepen personal experience through listening to others, working to understand the situation at hand and sharing their wisdom.

QUESTIONS FOR RELFECTION

1. Do you intentionally designate a short period of time to reflect each day? If so, how have you observed that it contributes to your life and work?

2. If not, and competing agendas have you bogged down, how can you successfully carve out or make adjustments to allow a time of quiet in your life?

3. What learning comes from your experience of reflection as a leader?

NOTES

5

THE EXPERIENCE OF INSIGHT TO WISDOM

"Wisdom is nothing but a preparation of the soul, a capacity, a secret act of thinking, feeling, and breathing thoughts of unity at every moment of life."
Herman Hesse

Reflection can train our minds and hearts to approach work out of a mission-driven, values-based perspective. It assists us to remain grounded in our purpose. Through reflection in our role as ministry leaders, we have the opportunity to engage in our work in such a manner as to recognize its influence on the people around us. If we appear centered, even in the face of conflict, we can approach tension-filled issues with a balanced point of view. A reflective approach to leadership expands our horizons and allows us to listen more clearly, enabling us to bring forward a fresh appreciation for our work and a new understanding for others' contributions by sharing a spirit of interdependence in the goals established and the vision set in living out the mission and values of the ministry.

LOOKING BACK, LEADING FORWARD

Ministry leaders are centered in their purpose, open to life-giving change, and demonstrate by their actions a reflective leadership style as a component of transformative leadership. Leaders such as these are ones who have encountered suffering and learned from it, have come to face the darkness and found deeper knowledge from it, have encountered the underworld and gained insight from it, and who have driven out their demons and found life anew. All leaders share responsibility for projecting either a spirit of light or the shadow of darkness.

Leaders must be cognizant of their actions, in as much as they foster a spirit of inner confidence or one of inner conflict. They are people who hold both formal and informal power and therefore must take note of what's going on inside their consciousness; otherwise, they can create more harm than good. All of us have a faithful companion within ourselves, which we call spirit. This companion is the source for us to practice the art of silence and reflection.

Those leaders who are invested in discovering the meaning of life's work through a personal conviction—a call—are known as reflective leaders. By relying on reflective models such as the Johari Window or the process steps of "experience, reflect, and respond," emerging leaders in Catholic long-term care and other mission-driven organizations can find merit through incorporating and applying these principles into their leadership style and lives.

REFLECTION IN CLINICAL PASTORAL EDUCATION

An additional way to use a reflective process is through clinical pastoral education (CPE), which is used in the training of hospital and hospice chaplains and spiritual care providers. In this educational model, students are asked to write detailed reflections on their experiences in pastoral or spiritual care, teasing out insights from them.

In chaplaincy and all pastoral-related services, using a compassionate listening approach, seeking to understand the patient's or resident's concern, and responding with observations of the experience with that person can prove to be helpful for both parties. This further reinforces the importance of reflective thinking for all ministry leaders, as it helps to create a process out of which a narrative can evolve for use in existing or future situations.

All reflective methods have practical application to aspects of cognitive behavioral therapy, which is defined as "an approach to problem-solving that helps persons understand thoughts and develop strategies to change behaviors." This behavioral health method contains insights on how an individual can have a "change in attitudes, values or beliefs that alters...self-expression. It occurs as a result of insight or behavioral achievement."

LISTENING DRAWS OUT INSIGHT

Transformational leaders bring a spirit of enthusiasm and insight to their work. They focus on listening to others and demonstrate trustworthy behavior. As transformational leaders, they encourage adaptability in work outcomes to ensure the safety and ongoing quality performance on behalf of the residents being cared for and, through their actions, manifest an expressed concern for others.

I find listening, understanding, and sharing to be useful stepping stones, as Teresa of Avila did, in finding the presence of God in our midst through a source of reflection.

Such an endeavor could also be considered for ministry leaders by using present work situations, assuming roles based upon the example, and applying a fish bowl circle environment, with the role players inside the circle and the remaining participants outside the circle to observe what they saw and experienced. The CPE model and other reflective models can create a new narrative of revelation for other disciplines more attuned with peer ministry or a small-group process when a team is involved. It has been used effectively throughout the health care industry and other professions and contains significant applicability for all leadership, including senior management.

FROM EXPERIENCE TO UNDERSTANDING

Transitioning with an example from the secular world of leadership, a 2014 position paper titled "Future Trends in Leadership Development" indicated that the pace of change happens rapidly in our society and world. While this reference was applied to the world of business, it also corresponds to the quick-paced health care environment and ever-changing regulatory world of long-term care. The paper identified a present challenge in how we tend to think about professional development: overemphasis on developing competencies (i.e., skills, abilities, and behaviors) and not enough focus on the relationship between experience and understanding.

The application of a parable for use in a ministry setting could easily complement the aforementioned quote. In Luke's gospel, Jesus tells the disciples "...no one pours new wine into old wineskins. Otherwise, the new wine will burst the skins, and it will be spilled, and the skins will be ruined. Rather, new wine must be poured into fresh wineskins."

Ministry leaders have the opportunity to incorporate both thoughts into their reflections. In both cases, there is personal growth and the opportunity to experience that which gives refreshment and life.

KNOWING OURSELVES TO LEAD OTHERS

In further addressing reflective models, the late Donald Schon, an educational consultant, and the late Chris Argyris, an organizational development specialist, were instrumental in developing a reflective application referred to as "the artistry of knowing," which referred to the ability to reflect on our actions as a means of learning more about ourselves, our professions, and the world around us. It requires us to be conscious of our emotions and behaviors, using them to grow our understanding.

Aspects of this reflective practice can be interpreted further. As Schon has suggested, there are notions of understanding our behavior as *reflection-in-action* and *reflection-on-action*. Reflection-in-action taps into our ability to access our emotions in order to respond to a situation, while reflection-on-action is an analysis of our response after the event has occurred. Both of these concepts, while relatively forthright, can provide us with a perspective of coming to better appreciate our own styles of motivation and action.

These reflections are then used by the practitioner in exploring a greater appreciation for their previous actions. They also gain a deeper insight on how they could have responded in a different manner. Aspects of this "reflection-on-action" practice appear to possess similarities to the written reflection utilized in clinical pastoral education and a reflective thinking method when used in case applications. These varied approaches draw upon a reflective element that engages the participant to pause and reflect on their actions, which are frequently underscored by their values and behavior.

LOOKING INWARD AT THE UNKNOWN

Ministry leaders can find benefits in using a reflective approach to their personal life and work experience, from which they have an increased learning gained from their experience. They have acquired a further understanding of how their beliefs, attitudes and values influence their actions, personal insight and growth. The areas of personal, organizational, and community identified earlier in this book have relevance here. In becoming a reflective leader, you will find that you're more attuned to others, both inside the organization and outside its walls, so as to engage and be present in a fashion that says, *"We care and are committed to serving this community."* It is important to recognize that when engaging in any self-reflection, an individual needs to be open to entering further into the unknown area of the "self," as previously referred to in the discussion of the Johari Window. It is from these unchartered waters that a person may experience darkness from what is found, but also find the inner strength to go beyond the shadows and into the light of new self-learning, which is a particularly important skill for leaders to possess. Reflective practice can guide all professionals toward providing greater leadership to their team and those they serve.

Ministry leaders need to integrate their reflective skills into the experience of day-to-day work. In practicing the reflective process of "experience, reflect, and respond" when applied to an encounter, leaders may find a new perspective for themselves that contributes to the ever-changing journey associated with being a wise leader.

GOING FURTHER INTO SELF-UNDERSTANDING

Another way of coming to know yourself as a ministry leader is to be cognizant of what is actually going on around you throughout the day. Being aware of your feelings and surroundings and all that such awareness encompasses allows the leader to be more readily appreciative and attuned to the milieu in which they work. Circumstances, situations, and issues that leaders encounter change rapidly and to varying degrees of personal challenge, but the actual cultural environment often remains the same.

Addressing our feelings about our experiences is very important for leaders. Feelings motivate our energy, and though we frequently cannot control the way feel about something, we can decide how to utilize those feelings in how we respond.

Responding to these feelings and experiences can be as process-driven as the method of "experience, reflect, respond" employed by the participants of the Roots of Caring program. In long-term care ministry, leaders need to be able to parse out their own issues and concerns that may overshadow or have undue influence in their discernment and decision making.

BEING PRESENT IN THE STRUGGLE

When ministry leaders assume the posture of being present to a challenging situation, there is an encounter that occurs between themselves and others. It is frequently unspoken, but the very act of being there gives rise to the witness that a committed leader can make a difference through their presence. This can be viewed by the employees as the leader listening to them, working to understand the problem and searching to find a way to share a response that can adequately address their concern, even when not being able to change the course of the outcome.

In these cases, the ministry leaders demonstrate through word and deed the ability to journey with their entire facility staff by struggling with the dilemma and suffering their own anxiety, while providing a vision of hope for all concerned. In good times and in bad times, the effective ministry leader is there. These leaders can have a profound influence in shaping the culture of the facility. Building upon the religious sponsors' identified mission and values they navigate the vision moving forward, fortified with the knowledge and experience that helps staff make sense of their own behavior and that of others in the organization.

In Catholic health care, we also find a welcome home for the exploration of the realm of spirituality. When people suffer physically, they are more susceptible to struggle spiritually as well. As a result, those who are suffering tend to reflect on their own lives, questioning their understanding of truth.

PRESENCING

As identified in Chapter One, the fast-paced changes of today's health care by those intimately engaged in the ministry are deeply affected by the ever-pressing issues of the social environment and the impacting quality of care and cost of care on residents and family members associated with long-term care. Believing that life is sacred from conception until natural death, Catholic long-term care organizations work to fulfill this moral tenet through personal, compassionate care of those they serve. This act has been referred to as *presencing*—a portmanteau of *presence* and *sense*—which is used to described leaders who are able to shift their consciousness to meet the demands of various situations.

This act of presencing occurs when a ministry leader sees themselves as a spiritual leader of the entire organization—not in the way that those in pastoral care do, but in a manner of caring for the whole facility staff. A parallel style called "spiritual leadership" can be defined as a model in which leaders actions are enmeshed with their values. These leaders tend to communicate integrity, vision, mission, enthusiasm, courage, and service to those they lead.

In bringing this chapter to conclusion, I do so with the realization of having identified numerous resources that can sustain ministry leaders in becoming reflective leaders. Dear reader, I hope you reach a perspective that provides you with a discovery point, a new insight, or epiphany in your work and ministry as you pursue becoming a reflective leader.

In Chapter 6, I will describe the experiences of the Roots of Caring students in more detail and discuss the process of the program.

QUESTIONS FOR REFLECTION

1. What fosters growth in your leadership style?

2. As referenced in this chapter, how are you an active "presence" to your organization?

3. What insight have you experienced as a leader in reading and reflecting on this book?

NOTES

6

REFLECTIONS ON THE FORMATION PROGRAM

"We will be known forever by the tracks we leave."
Dakota, Native America Sioux

We now come to the final part of this book. Picking up from Chapter One, this now becomes the other end of the bookends that draw together the experience of the Roots of Caring graduates. Chapter 2–5 have drawn upon the rich experience of leaders from both spiritual and secular arenas and their personal encounter with reflection that brings forth awareness, knowledge, and human development. It is from these past leaders that we owe a debt of gratitude for their insight and wisdom passed down for other generations of leaders to seek and find their own diamond in the rough.

In my introduction, I stated that twenty-five graduates, the majority of whom are lay women and men, of the Roots of Caring leadership formation program had previously indicated their desire for ongoing formation. As a response to that desire, I began developing a continuing formation program, which included an intensive seminar held November 1–2, 2016, and a schedule of assignments to be completed thereafter. The program participants would remain in contact with me as a means of turning in and discussing their assignments. The main objective of the intensive was to establish a solid groundwork for participants in reflective thinking. The extended engagement for participants throughout the remainder of November 2016 would enable them to further apply their learned experience using reflection methods. It was out of my own experience and use of these reflective skills that I became cognizant of what was necessary for these emerging leaders to further ensure the continuous viability and sustainability of the Catholic long-term care ministry.

Nine graduates from first and second cohorts chose to participate in the continuing formation experience. While they previously identified reasons for their participation (as indicated in Chapter One), they also wanted to acquire hands-on experience applying the reflective-thinking process of "experience, reflect, and respond" to case situations presented and discussed with them.

My belief for pursuing this inquiry was threefold, based upon my thirty–one years of experience in Catholic health care leadership. First, through ongoing formative experiences, leaders have the opportunity to be more open, expand their horizons, and, thereby, be a positive influence on their own thinking. Secondly, through engagement with peers who share similar yet distinct encounters with staff, residents, and family members in their respective facilities, they can learn from one another and expand their decision-making abilities. Thirdly, exposure to the concept of reflection could broaden their reflective skills and, with practice, bring new insight to their lives and issues they encounter in their work as ministry leaders.

OVERVIEW OF THE INTENSIVE SCHEDULE

During the two-day intensive, participants engaged in eight forty-five-minute sessions. I selected the topics for the intensive by building upon the pre-program survey results and the participants' experience in the Roots of Caring program. Several of these sessions were content-based and included worksheets to be used for the participants' personal application, reflection, and discussion. These topics were "Values," "Catholic Social Teaching," "Catholic Identity/ Parables," and "Reflective Leadership."

I created resource materials and activities that would expand on participants' learning from the Roots of Caring program. I wanted to ground these emerging leaders in applying a reflection process throughout the ongoing formation experience that would be user friendly for them. I did this by incorporating activities that necessitated pondering before completing the worksheets on values, Catholic social teaching, or parable application. For the fourth topic, reflective leadership, I presented a case application and walked through it step-by-step so participants could observe, participate in, and gain new insights from the reflective method.

Sessions five through seven of the intensive seminar contained case studies to which participants applied the learned reflective method. In each of these three sessions, one participant brought a case with them, and the group worked together to process it. This provided participants an opportunity to use a long-term care experience, which they could identify with, and get experience utilizing the reflection method. By applying reflective leadership skills, participants were given an opportunity to pause and meditate upon their own experience. They were also able to increase their personal awareness of how various aspects of the method provided insight for them and developed a perspective that had not been previously present in their leadership style.

In the eighth and final session of the intensive seminar, participants were asked to complete a self-assessment sheet, which they would use to rate and respond to several questions about the experience each of them had during the two-day intensive. Participants were also instructed to use a case worksheet and the "experience, reflect, and respond" method in identifying a case involving themselves and a staff member, resident, or family member. Each of the participants was asked to complete a total of three case worksheets and forward them to me. Participants were also asked to complete an identical 15 question values-based post-program survey for me to ascertain observations and insights based upon the participants' responses both before the program began and after they had completed it.

Everything that I taught and discussed with the participants was a means to guide them toward being able to answer these two questions:

1. What did they take away from the experience?
2. Would they recommend the intensive seminar for future graduates of the Roots of Caring program?

THE DETAILED PLAN

Upon arrival, participants were provided with a one-page schedule that outlined the sessions planned for November 1-2, 2016. On November 1, we gathered in the conference center and, following a brief introduction and prayer, reviewed the schedule the participants had received the previous day and outlined the format of our time together for the intensive seminar. I reiterated the purpose of the intensive seminar—namely, to foster and develop a process of reflection by which participants could reflect on new ideas presented or modify those thoughts already held by them as a means of experiencing personal insight and new learning into their leadership styles.

I then provided an overview of the project, which included the pre-survey and participant data sheet, theory and praxis content during the intensive seminar, case study usage, and application of reflective thinking and a self-assessment. Once participants returned home, they were to use the reflective methods they learned to complete cases they submitted to me for the remainder of the month.

Finally, participants were asked to complete and submit a post-program survey, which included asking them about their overall experience of participating in the project and if they would recommend the intensive seminar format to future Roots of Caring graduates as a continuing formation encounter.

SESSION TOPIC SELECTIONS

I chose the topics of "Values," "Catholic Social Teaching," and "Catholic Identity-Gospel Parables" because the Roots of Caring program provided a foundational overview of these three themes. In this continuing formation experience, I delved further into each of these three topics and developed reflective activities for participants to engage in throughout the intensive seminar. The key to this was an additional presentation and activity on the reflective process, which provided participants an opportunity to apply the process within the context of a case study example. Each of these topics directly contributed to applying the reflective process by naming the situation and circumstances (i.e., the context) you are addressing, clarifying which social values enter into the mix, identifying any religious themes or scriptural meaning that has bearing on the case, and taking time to assemble the pieces of the process, review them, reflect, and identify possible outcomes of the case. By using this methodology, I believed that insights or transformative experiences could more readily emerge and further contribute to the group discussion in processing the case.

The intensive seminar's purpose was to expose participants to concepts of reflective leadership. It was in their musings of the first three sessions on Values, Catholic Social Teaching, and Catholic Identity-Parables that they became more comfortable with the reflective process emerging through quiet time, followed by small and large group discussion. It is from this formative experience that participants were then exposed to a fourth session on the reflective process. A brief presentation was made, followed by my review of a case applying the reflective framework of "experience, reflect, and respond."

SESSION FORMAT & MATERIALS

The format of each session provided a familiar workshop style for participants to learn as they had done in Roots of Caring. In the first four sessions, I made presentations prior to their activity engagement. In sessions five, six, and seven, they worked as a group processing cases based upon their experiences and encounters with staff, residents, or family members. In the eighth and final session, they participated in a self-assessment of their intensive seminar experience. Each session provided an opportunity for the participants to engage in discussion both with the larger group and in smaller groups.

The participants practiced applying value-based concepts while learning the reflective process as a way to promote reflective skill development through participation in a group process. Case studies were employed to see how new insights and observations could be transformed into results that had taken place during the intensive seminar and when they returned home. By engaging participants in this project, they had an opportunity to learn and use a framework of the reflective process to explore cases, take time to gather their thoughts and share insights with one another in a comfortable, quiet atmosphere.

Having identified my purpose for each session, I will now describe the content that provided the supportive structure for the sessions and enabled participants to engage in the overall intensive seminar process and project.

Tuesday, November 1, 2016: Sessions One–Five

Session One: Values

In this module, I addressed how we come to garner our beliefs, attitudes, and values throughout our lives. There was a discussion of the types of values we are exposed to, including personal, family, social, spiritual, and material. We then engaged in a conversation on the Carmelite values that permeate the culture of the long-term care ministries.

A segment of this first session was dedicated to an activity titled "Knowing My Context." I presented it as a way of drawing the participants into identifying their personal histories and taking time to reflect upon those values that have emerged in their lives based upon their life journeys.

I provided an example of my own context prior to asking them to begin their activity. A worksheet was then provided for them to document their insights and reflections, which outlined five aspects:

1. Family origin
2. Family faith experience
3. Culture characteristics
4. Education & adult life
5. Behaviors that reflect my values

The field of social sciences has provided us a rich background that offers 5 W's to be considered when processing our personal knowledge in context:

1. Family origin asks the question of *"Who* am I?"
2. Faith experience asks the question of *"What* is my religious/spiritual journey?"
3. Culture characteristics asks the question of *"Where* did my heritage originate?"
4. Education & adult life asks the question of *"Why* did I follow the path to where I am today?" and the question of
5. *"When* have I observed my personal value(s) and action(s) in sync or colliding in life?"

We discussed the activity and made analogies to St. Teresa of Avila and Mother Angeline's calls to service. For this comparison, participants referred to handouts that identified the four Carmelite values and the seven key characteristics of Mother Angeline.

A two-page reflective handout titled "Carmelite Ministries Four Core Values" was distributed. They were to address how they listen, understand, and share as ministry leaders in the Carmelite system. They were asked to take time on the evening of November 1 to apply this approach to their experience of redemptive suffering, and we would discuss this as a group on the following morning.

Session Two: Catholic Social Teaching

In this session, participants reflected on how to appreciate the circumstances in which the encyclicals or pastoral letters were written as messages of hope for our world. We reviewed a brief document from the Catholic Health Association of the United States titled "A Shared Statement of Identity for the Catholic Health Ministry." They were divided into groups and provided with a large worksheet that identified the author, year, major issues, and ideas of papal encyclicals promulgated between 1891 and 1987.

Each group was assigned 3 or 4 encyclicals. They were asked to discuss the circumstances in which each of these documents were written, reflect on what they identified, and use the "Catholic Health Association Shared Statement" handout to identify one or more of the seven social values that complement the encyclicals. The importance of this activity was to raise the participants' social consciousness of the situations presented and the era in which it occurred. This experience was used as an example of reflection to demonstrate that, as people of faith, they can influence systems thinking in the ministries where they serve.

Session Three: Catholic Identity and Scripture Application

In this session, participants engaged in an exercise titled "Catholic Identity—Telling the Story." We reviewed the Hebrew and Christian message of story and applied Sacred Scripture by using several healing parables of Jesus as a way to reflect on what was happening in the story. Again, divided into small groups, they were assigned one of the following four parables: Cure of a Woman with a Hemorrhage (Mk 5:25-34), Cure of the Leper (Mk 1:40-45), Two Blind Men (Mt 20:29-34), or The Good Samaritan (Lk 10:25-27). They were directed to read the assigned story and reflect on the following questions individually and then in their small group:

1. What's going on in the story?
2. Which values are present in the story narrative?
3. Where do you see examples of this story in our lives today?

They used a handout to assemble personal and group notes, and each group chose a spokesperson to summarize and share their collected thoughts.

Session Four: Reflective Reflection and Case Application
In this session, participants were introduced to a model of reflective leadership. I gave a brief presentation and provided a handout that described the steps of the model in greater detail, which I discussed with the group. I presented a case study titled "Michael," and I walked the group through the case step-by-step while leading the process and observing how the participants were engaging, pondering, and responding to it.

I provided a reflective thinking worksheet that included a model for participants to reference as they engaged in group work. We used the "Experience" section of the worksheet to identify what was going on in the case as it related to relationship, cultural, social aspects and for the participants to document a brief statement that captured their own thoughts. In the "Reflect" segment of the worksheet, participants were asked to assess the previous statement in terms of values, Catholic social teaching principles, scripture quotes or parables. In the "Response" section of the handout, participants were asked to document thoughts and insights from the case that influenced them as a leader and to state what they learned from this experience.

Session Five: Group Case Application by Participants
In session five, the participants were to be divided again into small groups, but they requested to remain as a whole group as

they processed the cases together as a way to share and learn the process from one another, and I supported the request A case study was provided, and they processed the case using the reflective method

Wednesday, November 2, 2016: Sessions Six–Eight

<u>Sessions Six and Seven: Case Application by Participants</u>
The opening discussion centered on insights from their previous evening's Carmelite values activity on redemptive suffering. Immediately following this discussion, we transitioned back into group case application using two more cases. Each of these cases, respectively, was engaged in by the group during the remainder of session six and for session seven.

<u>Session Eight: Participant Self-Assessment</u>
In the eighth session, they were provided a self-assessment of the continuing formation intensive seminar. They were asked to take some quiet time to reflect on their encounter together and respond to three questions:

1. How was the overall experience of the intensive seminar for you? Please describe.
2. On a scale of 1–5, please rate your understanding of the reflective thinking process.
3. What key learning(s) or insights have come about for you during the intensive seminar?

Intensive Seminar Experience: Conclusion
Once I had collected the completed self-assessments, I reiterated how the remainder of the month of November would proceed with three individual cases to be completed by them once a week.

Participants came to adopt reflective leadership method as a valuable process for themselves as leaders, acquired a clearer sense of how reflection improves their insight to everyday issues, and developed a deeper understanding of how it offered an informed, values-based perspective on organizational work life and culture.

Through the course of the intensive seminar, I observed the participants' willingness to embrace new ideas, be open to thoughtful discernment, and adapt to suggested changes—all of which points to a transforming experience beginning to emerge. Their insights oftentimes served as a learning experience for me. I was able to see how they connected the resource materials of the intensive seminar to the group case applications by using reflective thinking.

Through this engagement I have come to better appreciate my own depth of wisdom and that which I heard them speaking from their hearts. I realize wisdom such as this can remain untapped unless we seek out the opportunity that avails itself through quiet introspection, meditation, and reflection. I believe this is a seminal aspect of becoming a true ministry leader upon which all other components of our life and work merge and come together.

Results and Corresponding Discussion

In Chapter One, I presented an overview summary of the nine participants in the continuing education project. Using their data as background information I now present the findings of the pre-and post-program values survey.

The change in participants' responses to the fifteen values-based pre-program (October 2016) and post-program (end of November 2016) survey questions, using a five-point scale, indicated an overall positive learning outcome from the intensive seminar of November 1–2, 2016 and the project as a whole. The increase on a pre-post question to question comparison ranged from 7% to 26%, as identified in Figure 3. These results also demonstrated a combined increase in each of the subsets addressed in the narrative below.

	Topic of Discussion/Response	Pre-Score	Post-Score	% Change
1)	I extend hospitality to all those I encounter in my ministry.	4.3	4.6	+7%
2)	I demonstrate the dignity of persons in my actions as a leader.	4.2	4.6	+9%
3)	I manifest the Mission of the organization in my daily work.	4.2	4.7	+12%
4)	I encourage a spirit of compassion in the workplace.	3.8	4.8	+26%
5)	I act on behalf of justice issues for staff, residents and family members.	3.9	4.4	+13%
6)	I look to our organizational values as a guide in my decision making.	4.2	4.7	+12%
7)	I consider on how God is present in our facility.	4.1	4.7	+15%
8)	I act to alleviate discrimination of the aged and vulnerable elderly.	4.1	4.7	+15%
9)	I believe that caring for the elderly is a way to reduce human suffering.	4.4	5.0	+14%
10)	I support attending to the needs of the whole person; body, mind and spirit.	4.2	5.0	+19%
11)	I am mindful of organizational resource and use them wisely.	4.0	4.6	+15%
12)	I understand the experience of suffering as being wider than sickness.	4.1	4.4	+7%
13)	I reflect on the human condition of others when considering the common good.	3.7	4.6	+24%
14)	I engage in a thoughtful process when making integral decisions.	3.8	4.7	+24%
15)	I consider my work a Christian witness to those I serve in word and deed.	4.1	4.8	+17%

Figure 3. Change in Survey Responses from Pre-Program to Post-Program

Summary of Pre- and Post-Survey Results Observations

The questions identified statements that contributed to the core value assumptions of the Carmelite ministries. It was from my observations during the intensive seminar and assessment of these results that I found the previously stated outcomes of the project to be successful, experientially positive and spiritually beneficial.

The organizational, community, and personal dimensions fit in a compelling manner to the value questions responses and provide a means for elaborating on the role of emerging ministry leaders. The ability of a leader to care for another person demonstrates one's willingness to go outside oneself by possessing both the consciousness of mind and the ability to act in a caring manner. The art of caring can be life giving to others and promote a sense of self-worth. Leaders who care will oftentimes find their own self-esteem and relationships enhanced from the energy they derive in providing such selfless initiative.

This form of dedicated service is demonstrated by the inner values that a leader holds central to knowing who they are. This is imbedded in a leader who has identified their ability to understand the context in which they came into this life. Namely, understanding their family of origin, mores, culture, religious tradition, and social milieu from which they grew and developed as persons. When leaders reflect, and ponder on how they got from here to there, it is frequent that they have been enlightened by their past role models who, through their service to others, influenced them in shaping their beliefs, attitudes and values. This activity of understanding my context served as a valuable resource in setting the value stage for these leaders.

Organizational Dimension Results

Their combined *organizational dimension* response for the subset of questions 1-5 indicated a 0.5 increase from the 4.1 combined average score in the pre-program survey to the 4.6 combined average score in the post-program survey, which represents a 13% increase. These questions align with creating a climate of mutual trust and the desire and willingness of these leaders to promote a culture that fosters openness within the facility. They do this by encouraging a spirit of compassion, in acting justly and respectfully for all parties, through manifesting the mission in their actions and being hospitable to all who come to the facility. An organization is as good as its' leader. A leader's credibility is based upon the consistent values driven behavior that is demonstrated to others. This behavior demonstrates the inner workings of the leader themselves and enables others to build their reliance and expectations of the leaders' actions, decisions and vision for the ministry. This is essential in building a healthy organizational culture.

Community Dimension Results

Their combined *community dimension* response from the subset of questions 6-10 indicated a 0.6 increase from the 4.2 combined average score in the pre-program survey to the 4.8 combined average score in the post-program survey, which represents a 14% increase. This shows leaders who inspire a positive perspective both in and outside the organization. They animate the mission and give meaning to the work of the ministry for themselves and others. This contributes to a deeper understanding of being called a ministry leader. Assuming a leadership position in a Carmelite long-term care organization necessitates a commitment to respecting the elderly community in a non-discriminate manner. It also means seeing each individual as a person whose beliefs, abilities and skills that have contributed to who they are and how they see the greater world of work. It means, as the leader, being cognizant of God's presence at work and of holistic needs being addressed in service to residents, families and staff.

Personal Dimension Results

Their combined *personal dimension* response from the subset of questions 11-15 indicated a 0.7 increase from the 3.9 combined average score in the pre-program survey to the 4.6 combined average score in the post-program survey, which represents an 18% increase and reflects the leaders' desire to create an environment where the expression of feelings can be revealed. This type of leader is able to effectively express warmth and sensitivity when it is called for at work and shows that others are valued. In doing so, the leader encourages staff to consider the common good by care for others. This atmosphere animates the desire to improve oneself and to encourage others to do the same. Healthiness of body, mind and spirit contributes to reducing stress by enhancing self-esteem, improves personal energy and contributes to an expanded appreciation of life's investments.

Leadership by Facing the Challenge of Suffering

Ministry leaders, through their experience, know the challenge of bearing the pain in personal and professional life. Such thoughtful decision-making actions are imperative for leaders, so that by their actions, staff can reflect the reality of caring for those who are aging, physically sick and/or simultaneously suffering emotionally or spiritually.

Additionally, in identifying with redemptive suffering, leaders' can demonstrate how they bear the pain when faced with a human resource, operational, or financial dilemma that is complex and necessary to be resolved for the good of the ministry.

My own experience of being a ministry leader meant taking the risk of moving from focusing on myself to paying attention to the ongoing needs of others. This leg of the journey demanded a self-reflective view of who I am and what I am called to do.

In being committed to ministry leadership, each of us comes face to face with all of life's challenges and realizes how they pull on our strengths and weaknesses. We must be open to trust in the transforming power of God in our lives and maintain a visionary spirit in the service of others.

Values Reflection: Moving from Experience to Insight

Leaders who embody inner strength from personal, organizational and community aspects of spiritual leadership will become true ministry leaders. This pre-post values survey summary has demonstrated in the results that a transforming experience had occurred, and their leadership style was changed by their engagement in this study.

They were provided a Carmelite values worksheet and asked to reflect on a situation they had encountered which corresponded to the values. By doing so, they began to notice how to interpret the values reflection. I observed them beginning to understand a relationship between what was being revealed through the exercise and the insight that came with sharing their wisdom with one another. Again, these were useful steps in being reflective.

My Observations on the Value of Hospitality

They demonstrated a welcoming spirit as a sound way to model this value in the facility. Through their daily work, they see and observe the lives they affect by their actions and realize that respecting and caring for one another, especially for the most vulnerable, aged, and infirm is part and parcel of their calling. Their responses complement their "Knowing My Context" perspectives on dedicated family eldercare and committed support for one another. They saw and experienced this loving care in their homes growing up and have come to value this giving of self in service to others in their work.

My Observations on the Value of Shared Commitment

They identified teamwork and mutual respect as being essential to accomplish the goals of the facility. Their responses parallel their "Knowing My Context" insights of family first in the spirit of one for all and all for one. They are willing to place other priorities first and work for a common vision. This is familiar behavior for these individuals and a positive experience they were exposed to in their youth. Their insights demonstrate the ability to sustain and transfer this sense of shared commitment from family origins into adult work settings.

My Observations on the Value of Compassion

Participants demonstrated a compassionate spirit through availability and kindness to the residents, families and staff. They realize their presence makes a difference in the facility. Being there to comfort others is a prevalent aspect these individuals experienced in their family systems and have incorporated into their values formation as adults.

My Observations on the Value of Sanctity of Life

In the Carmelite Sisters' ministries, redemptive suffering is understood as recognizing that sickness, suffering and death are potential occasions of experiencing God. The following paraphrases the participants' collective thoughts on the value of Sanctity of Life. They indicated that emotional pain is important to identify and provide comfort to people who are in sorrow.

In numerous instances, they tried to put themselves in the residents' place and were actively listening and physically present as a way of being supportive. They believe you never give up on faith and hope. Listening, not speaking, may be the only thing needed. God put this in their path for a reason, and suffering can be seen as an opportunity to experience God in their midst. My observation is their insights are well thought out, and, in some ways, speak to the unspoken experience of suffering they too have been confronted with in life.

Reflecting on these difficult experiences such as dementia, chronic illness, and end of life allowed participants to encounter suffering from the perspective of a caregiver. Pope John Paul II wrote, "Every individual, through personal suffering, constitutes not only a small part of that world but at the same time that world is present…as an infinite and unrepeatable entity." This bond, unique unto itself, peels away all peripheral concerns and brings into the spotlight the very meaning of life and its cherished history. Such keen awareness, if enacted by ministry leaders, contributes to their call to serving others and demonstrates the core importance of compassion.

<u>Going on the Journey: Listening and Patience</u>

These leaders acknowledged the importance to listen and be patient with those who are sick. They have been close to suffering and identified the gift of gratitude for their health while walking with another who is less fortunate. The learning comes through the reflection and the merit of this journey. As persons of faith, they realized that suffering can make them stronger and not everyone gets to be present at these cherished times.

In many faith traditions death is viewed as a release from agony and sadness. It can also be understood as a time of transition and transformation from this life to the next. Sharing these experiences brought about life-changing perspectives in the participants regarding the journey of death and dying.

I observed this particular reflective experience to impact them and draw them into a deeper engagement with the meaning of suffering. I heard during the discussion that several of them had a life changing, transforming experience of what suffering felt like and how it brought them closer to seeing God at work through others. In such an experience, they came to see the struggle, healing and personal growth as part of the journey of life.

Overall, I see through their reflections of listening, understanding and sharing how they have demonstrated that building upon their own values-based experiences has reinforced their ability to develop, grow and change as adults. Working and leading in a Catholic long-term care environment or other mission-driven organization becomes an unqualified fit for these leaders.

These activities of "Knowing My Context" and values-based applications were essential to set the stage for participants to rely upon their reflective skills from life experiences. It is from this bedrock of recognizing and appreciating where each of us came from that I transitioned into a section on Catholic Social Teaching, an applied approach.

Reflective Activity on Catholic Social Teaching

For the module on Catholic Social Teaching, participants reviewed a CHA document on the constitutive elements of Catholic health care. Working in small groups, they engaged in an activity that included a handout describing a series of encyclicals written from 1891 to 1991. Details concerning major challenges and messages each encyclical addressed were provided to them. Participants were asked to discuss 3-4 of the encyclicals in their groups and to apply one or more of the Catholic health care constitutive elements to each document.

Catholic Social Teaching Activity Summary: Group 1

One group reviewed *After Forty Years,* which addressed the Great Depression and identified the constitutive elements of Act on Behalf of Justice, Promote the Common Good. They also reviewed *Christianity and Social Progress,* whose major challenges were technological advances, and again referenced several of the previous elements on justice, stewardship, common good and added care of the poor and vulnerable. They readily identified with this document and the 1961 concerns of technology and the implications on U.S. health care at that time. Their final document to review was *Peace on Earth,* which addressed the arms race and the threat of nuclear war. Once again, Justice, the Common Good and Promote and Defend Human Dignity were identified as being applicable, and their discussion focused on the impact of war, the senseless loss of life and the aftermath of such an endeavor worldwide. I observed this activity drew them into intense discussion and appeared to stretch their thinking on the topics inasmuch as reflecting on the themes, connecting the issues and integrating the constitutive elements into the mix brought about a multitasking process for them to encounter.

Catholic Social Teaching Activity Summary: Group 2

A second group reviewed *Pastoral Constitution on the Church and Modern World*, which challenged the younger generations' questioning traditional values and identified Attend to the Whole Person and Dignity of the Person. They shared perspectives on the emerging culture chaos of the sixties in the United States and the need to balance wisdom of the past with experiences of the present. They also discussed *The Development of Peoples*, which concerned the widening gap of the rich and poor worldwide. They identified compatible elements of Promote the Common Good and Care of the Poor and Vulnerable. Their discussion was around women, children and the elderly and their experience of financial and social challenges, such as health care insurance, that faced these groups both then and now.

Finally, they documented observations on *A Call to Action on the 80th Anniversary of Rerum Novarum* and *Justice in the World*, both written in 1971. They saw the elements of Acting on Behalf of Justice and to Promoting Human Dignity as being significant in the context of working in Communion with the Church. Their insights addressed job availability and disparity of educational opportunities within various socio-economic groups at that time. Discussion of health care access and insurance became relevant to their dialogue and they found this reflective exercise helpful.

Catholic Social Teaching Activity Summary: Group 3

The third and final group chose to focus their time discussing *On Human Work*, which addressed capitalism and communism and the treatment of workers as production instruments. Their sole element identified was Promote and Defend Human Dignity. Their comments were health care based and included pay scales then and now, differences in male-female employment, and upward mobility and seemingly unfair expectations of paid positions versus hourly positions concerning the number of hours on the job. This group's energy was cathartic in identifying with our broken health care delivery system and the response needed to make affordable health care available to everyone.

<u>My Observations on the Catholic Social Teaching Activity</u>
In summary, I observed the rich discussion from each of the groups as providing a social perspective to reflect on and discuss real life situations on a large scale while incorporating Catholic health care elements into the activity. As a whole, they realized the challenge of capitalism in America was oftentimes at odds with the social teaching of the Church and indicated this experience was very enlightening for them when they introduced the topic of health care into the equation.

They came to realize that a Catholic health care provider stands as a witness to the Christian mission and the values that it represents. Also, that organizational witness stems from personal, interpersonal and social dimensions of life. As emerging leaders, they could see that their role is to champion this cause for justice in health care.

<u>Catholic Identity and Scripture Application</u>
Following my presentation, they again got into small groups. They were assigned four Gospel stories and asked to identify the following:

1. What's going on in the story?
2. Which values are present in the story narrative?
3. Which behaviors stand out in the story?
4. Where do they see examples of this story in their lives today?

Cure of a Woman with a Hemorrhage (Mark 5:24- 34)

The first group discussed the Cure of a Woman with a Hemorrhage from Mark 5:24–34 and shared that this woman is ill, poor, vulnerable, and in despair, but her faith and determination kept her going. Jesus' own awareness is that one is in need among the many that were present to him. The values they saw present were care of the poor, redemptive suffering, and compassion. The behaviors they identified with were courage and determination, fear, questioning, self-awareness and inspiration. In their lives today, they cited examples of caring for those who are elderly, at times vulnerable, and in need of an advocate and their role to ensure safety and respect for them.

Cure of the Leper (Mark 1:40–45)

Group two addressed the parable of Cure of the Leper from Mark 1:40–45 and shared this story: Jesus cured a leper and told him not to tell anyone, but he did and ruined it for Jesus and everybody else. The values present are compassion, hope, healing and sanctity of life. The actions present are asking for help, outspoken, broken confidence, sorrow and compassion. Examples of this today in work are gossip, or a charitable act done quietly, but later disclosed to all staff, and now everybody wants something, and no one believed without seeing a miracle—a lack of faith. This group encountered new personal challenges while working to maintain confidentiality and needing to find a balanced resolve to the issue of integrity being faced within the facility.

Two Blind Men (Matthew 20:29–34)

The third group reviewed the parable of Two Blind Men from Matthew 20:29–34 and shared what's going on: Jesus is healing several men who cannot see. Values present in this narrative are care of the poor and vulnerable and compassionate whole person care. Behaviors present were similar to some residents acting out in a time of need because they could not see what has to be done in order to make the resident comfortable. The residents' actions appeared to serve as a desire to alleviate their pain. In this situation, I observed the group's ability to see through the residents' actions, go below the surface and take the time to reflect. They saw this is where wisdom can emerge in making an insightful and compassionate decision.

The Good Samaritan (Luke 10:25–27)

Finally, group four was given the parable of The Good Samaritan from Luke 10:25–27. They indicated the story portrayed a scholar questioning Jesus about the law and Jesus uses the story of the Good Samaritan to explain to him, who is my neighbor. The values present here are to treat others the way you want to be treated, sanctity of life and compassion. Actions or behaviors present in the story are the priest and Levite, whom you would expect to show compassion, did not, but instead the isolated traveler stopped, provided care and money to continue the person's care to recovery. We see this today by taking in residents on Medicaid who have been denied acceptance into other facilities, and residents who arrive without any personal belongings and we proceed to acquire clothing for them. It is all about their dignity and treating others the way you want to be treated.

My Observations of the Gospel Story Activity by Participants

The intention of this exercise was to engage and draw out the values and corresponding behaviors that parallel Jesus' actions by identifying with what is expected of a Christian witness today and, in particular, a ministry leader. I found them connecting to this activity and seeing the benefit of applying Gospel stories to the meaning of their work and ministry today.

Reflective Leadership: Case Study Activity

We began session four, which was on reflective leadership and the reflective-thinking process, with a presentation accompanied by a sample case study titled "Michael" that I led for the participants as way for them to gain exposure to the method. At the conclusion of the presentation, the participants worked as a group to engaged in another case. The sample case of "Michael" is provided below, followed by a table summarizing the participants' responses to this case using the reflective-thinking process of "Experience, Reflect, Respond."

Reflective Leadership Case: Michael

Michael is a 35-year-old Nursing Assistant at Happy Meadows Skilled Care Facility. He has worked there for 6 years on the night shift. He is married and his wife, Eileen, works the day shift in the Dietary Department of the Facility. Together they have 3 children from previous marriages. The children are in middle or high school and appear to be good kids. Eileen and Michael intentionally work alternating shifts so one of them is available for the children.

Michael's new supervisor, Marian, wants him to shift his schedule and work when Eileen does during the day. Michael has explained to her the reason he works nights and Eileen days. Marian has said she understands but continues to suggest to Michael that working days would be more conducive to the needs of the department. Michael is beginning to feel the pressure from this and has spoken with Eileen about him looking for a similar position in another facility where he could work nights without being challenged.

Michael's peers in the department have "gotten word" of the situation and are beginning to act out on behalf of Michael. Marian finds night staff coming in late or calling in sick; thereby necessitating her dependence on Michael to remain on nights. Everyone seems to be in a dilemma so how do we move forward?

EXPERIENCE—Identify what's going on in the case in terms of…	
Relationship issues Well liked; [has] support of peers	
Cultural Context Family priority; open communication; desire to maintain status quo	
Social Milieu Subtle duress; power issues; influence	
Write what you determine into a short summary statement:	Michael is in conflict of family vs. work. He had a desire to find an acceptable resolution.
REFLECT— Assess the summary statement in terms of…	
Values Compassion, family, stability, respect, love	
CST Principles Attend to whole person; act on behalf of justice	
Scripture Quote Mt 13:44-53—Treasure hidden/pearl of value; fish good/bad LK 5-39—Old wire is better than new	
Parables: Hidden Treasure; Old and New	
RESPOND	
Identify thoughts, insights from the case that influence you as a leader:	Being adaptable; clear communication; be reflective; reduce colleagues' involvement; promote team spirit; walk in "my shoes"
Document what you have learned from this experience:	Michael is an informal leader and has respect for all. Be empathetic; promote peaceful resolve; win/win; my listening; adapting and support as leader; balance of human needs.

Figure 4. Reflective Leadership Case: Michael, Group Responses

My Observation of the Group in "Michael"

The participants were very attentive to my case-modeling approach using the reflective-thinking process designed for this intensive seminar. As I solicited input from the group, they were eager to contribute. I noted they were not judgmental about the supervisor, but they also felt the leader did not handle the situation well from the very beginning. They could readily identify with this case example, and that helped to make them more comfortable with the reflective-thinking process.

Self-Assessment Summary of the Intensive Seminar

In the eighth and final session of the intensive seminar, they received a one-page self-assessment handout that asked the following:

1. How was the overall experience?
2. How would you rate the intensive seminar on a scale of 1-5?
3. What key learning or insight came to you during the intensive seminar, and what was one insight for you as a ministry leader?

Responses regarding the overall experience were generally positive, with most rating the intensive seminar as "very good" or "exceptional." Participants felt as though they were able to better evaluate their own leadership qualities and improve their situational analysis and decision-making skills as a result of the experience. They felt the use of reflective leadership methods would allow them to address personal and professional events with more clarity and confidence, which benefits themselves as well as the residents, families, and employees with whom they work.

Overall, they found the experience to be a positive source of learning the reflective-thinking process, and it has provided them new insight into their ministry leadership.

CONCLUSION

I have found these outcomes have demonstrated participants' view of reflective leadership as a valuable concept for themselves. They have seen how being reflective can improve their insight into everyday issues in the ministry. Further, they have developed a deeper understanding and appreciation for the reflective process in its application to values based issues within their organizational work-life and culture.

My own experience of the entire project was an opportunity for me to personally grow and develop, along with them, in this learning journey and become more enlightened through my deeper spiritual awareness. I found myself being drawn into their discussions, and I observed, with great delight, their active engagement in the reflective-thinking process.

Through this project, I have come to better appreciate and understand their rich perspectives and views, and how, as the process unfolded, they seemed to build off one another throughout the group discussions. My own ideas led to new and enriched insights throughout the process. While each of them, myself included, found the intensive seminar exhausting, we also shared enthusiasm and energy with one another during the entire engagement. It became a real immersion experience. I observed a change in attitudes and greater openness to new decision-making approaches that involved identifying the experience, reflecting on it, and responding to the issue at hand.

Through it all, I renewed my own appreciation for reflective leadership and experienced how each part of the puzzle came together during the intensive seminar. Through our ongoing communication, both during the intensive and in the following weeks, we were able to create an environment of trust, support and encouragement for one another. I experienced a significant openness of mind and heart from them and myself, and I believe this contributed to the overall success of the intensive seminar and the project as a whole.

QUESTIONS FOR REFLECTION

1. What is your own experience of leadership development?

2. In your organization, do you perceive a need for formative experiences for your leaders? If so, what areas of concentration would your team benefit from?

3. How could aspects of this book effectively serve you and other leaders in your profession?

NOTES

APPENDIX

PRE- & POST-SURVEY QUESTIONS

How often do you incorporate the following practices into your ministry leadership?

Rate each of the following statements on a scale of 1–5, with 1 representing "Almost never" and 5 representing "Almost always."

1. I extend hospitality to all those I encounter in my ministry
2. I demonstrate the dignity of persons in my actions as a leader.
3. I manifest the Mission of the Organization in my daily work.
4. I encourage a spirit of compassion in the workplace.
5. I act on behalf of justice issues for staff, residents and family members.
6. I look to our organizational values as a guide in my decision making.
7. I consider on how God is present in our facility.
8. I act to alleviate discrimination of the aged and vulnerable elderly.
9. I believe that caring for the elderly is a way to reduce human suffering.
10. I support attending to the needs of the whole person; body, mind and spirit.
11. I am mindful of organizational resources and use them wisely.
12. I understand the experience of suffering as being wider than sickness.
13. I reflect on the human condition of others when considering the common good.
14. I engage in a thoughtful process when making integral decisions.
15. I consider my work a Christian witness to those I serve in word and deed.

KNOWING MY CONTEXT

Family Origins:

Family Faith Experience:

Culture Characteristics:

Education & Adult Life:

Behaviors That Reflect My Values:

REDEMPTIVE SUFFERING

Describe a situation you encountered in your own ministry when you listened to someone who was suffering?

Briefly explain how you understood his or her suffering:

What insight came to you through this experience of suffering that you could share?

CARMELITE CORE VALUES

Ministry leadership development reinforces personal exploration of one's own giftedness, call to service, and commitment to the mission and values of Catholic health care. Comprehensive study, spiritual reflection, integration of values in operations—in all these is an opening of God's grace. Leadership ministry strengthens persons for this critical role in Catholic long-term care.

St. Teresa of Avila was a 15th-century Carmelite mystic and reformer of the Carmelite movement (OCD). One of her writings, *Interior Castles,* was an autobiography of her journey and personal prayer. In Teresa's writings, the word *experience* is the opposite of *theory.* Experience is to know something for having lived it, felt it or gone through it. It is from the common, multiple life experiences, lights and shadows, victories and defeats, successes and disappointments, a good direction along the way or losing one's way that we are transformed.

Mother Angeline knew this when she founded the Carmelite Sisters for the Aged and Infirm in the 20th century. She, like Teresa, faced challenges, joys, and sorrows. Through her sustaining vision, reflective prayer life, and selfless commitment to others, she succeeded in bringing the elderly a life filled with hospitality and compassion while exemplifying sanctity of life for all and a shared commitment to the service of aged and infirm in the United States and Ireland.

Both of these women experienced suffering throughout their lives. Down through the centuries and generations it has been seen that in suffering there is concealed a particular power that draws a person interiorly close to Christ, a special grace, a life-changing experience that enables us to hear with new ears and see with new eyes. Such an experience is redemptive suffering.

In practicing reflective leadership, we come to observe that when we're reflective, we are inwardly listening. When we open our mind and heart to interpret the reflection, we begin to understand what meaning and message is being given to us. When we gently communicate our insight with others, we are sharing our wisdom.

CARMELITE CORE VALUES ACTIVITY

Hospitality (Wholistic Caring and Spiritual Care)

I listen-reflect on as…

I understand as…

I share as…

Sanctity of Life (RCD, Christian Witness, Redemptive Suffering)

I listen-reflect on as…

I understand as…

I share as…

Shared Commitment (Social Justice, Signs of the Times)

I listen-reflect on as…

I understand as…

I share as…

Compassion (Quality of Life, Kindness)

I listen-reflect on as…

I understand as…

I share as…

CATHOLIC SOCIAL TEACHING ACTIVITY

Latin Title: *Rerum Novarum*
English Translation: The Condition of Labor
Year of Pub.: 1891
Source: Pope Leo XIII
Major Challenges: Industrialization, urbanization, poverty
Major New Ideas or Message: "Family wage," workers' rights

Comments:

Latin Title: *Quadragesimo Ano*
English Translation: After Forty Years, or the Reconstruction of the Social Order
Year of Pub.: 1931
Source: Pope Pius XI
Major Challenges Addressed: Great Depression, communism and fascist dictatorships
Major New Ideas or Message: Subsidiarity as a guide to government interventions

Comments:

Latin Title: *Mater et Magistra*
English Translation: Christianity and Social Progress
Year of Pub.: 1961
Source: Pope John XXII
Major Challenges Addressed: Technological advances
Major New Ideas or Message: Global justice between rich and poor nations

Comments:

Latin Title: *Pacem in Terris*
English Translation: Peace on Earth
Year of Pub.: 1963
Source: Pope John XXII
Major Challenges Addressed: Arms race, the threat of nuclear war
Major New Ideas or Message: A philosophy of human rights and social responsibilities

Comments:

Latin Title: *Guadium et Spes*
English Translation: Pastoral Constitution on The Church in the Modern World
Year of Pub.: 1965
Source: Second Vatican Council
Major Challenges Addressed: Younger generations questioning traditional values
Major New Ideas or Message: Church must scrutinize external "signs of the times"

Comments:

Latin Title: *Popolorum Progressio*
English Translation: The Development of Peoples
Year of Pub.: 1967
Source: Pope Paul VI
Major Challenges Addressed: Widening gap between rich and poor nations
Major New Ideas or Message: "Development is the new word for peace"

Comments:

Latin Title: *Octogesima Adveniens*
English Translation: A Call to Action on the 80th Anniversary of *Rerum Novarum*
Year of Pub.: 1971
Source: Pope Paul VI
Major Challenges Addressed: Urbanization marginalizes vast multitudes
Major New Ideas or Message: Lay Catholics must focus on political action to combat injustices

Comments:

Latin Title: *Justitia in Mundo*
English Translation: Justice in the World
Year of Pub.: 1971
Source: Synod of Bishops
Major Challenges Addressed: Structural injustices and oppression inspire liberation movements
Major New Ideas or Message: "Justice … is a constitutive dimension of the preaching of the Gospel"

Comments:

Latin Title: *Envangelii Nuntiandi*
English Translation: Evangelization in the Modern World
Year of Pub.: 1974
Source: Pope Paul VI
Major Challenges Addressed: Cultural problems of atheism, secularism, consumerism
Major New Ideas or Message: Cultural problems of atheism, secularism, consumerism

Comments:

Latin Title: *Laborem Exercens*
English Translation: On Human Work
Year of Pub.: 1981
Source: Pope John Paul II
Major Challenges Addressed: Capitalism and communism treat workers as mere instruments of production
Major New Ideas or Message: Work is the key to the "social question" and to human dignity

Comments:

Latin Title: *Sollicitudo rei Socialis*
English Translation: On Social Concern
Year of Pub.: 1987
Source: Pope John Paul II
Major Challenges Addressed: Persistent underdevelopment, division of world into blocs
Major New Ideas or Message: "Structures of sin" are responsible for global injustices

Comments:

Latin Title: *Centesimus Annus*
English Translation: On the Hundredth Anniversary of *Rerum Novarum*
Year of Pub.: 1991
Source: Pope John Paul II
Major Challenges Addressed: Collapse communism in Eastern Europe
Major New Ideas or Message: Combat consumeristic greed in new "knowledge economy"

Comments:

GOSPEL STORIES OF HEALING

Cure of a Woman with a Hemorrhage (Mark 5:25–34)
There was a woman afflicted with hemorrhages for twelve years. She had suffered greatly at the hands of many doctors and had spent all that she had. Yet she was not helped but only grew worse. She had heard about Jesus and came up behind him in the crowd and touched his cloak.

She said, "If I but touch his clothes, I shall be cured."

Immediately her flow of blood dried up. She felt in her body that she was healed of her affliction. Jesus, aware at once that power had gone out from him, turned around in the crowd and asked, "Who has touched my clothes?"

But his disciples said to him, "You see how the crowd is pressing upon you, and yet you ask, 'Who touched me?'"

And he looked around to see who had done it. The woman, realizing what had happened to her, approached in fear trembling. She fell down before Jesus and told him the whole truth. He said to her, "Daughter, your faith has saved you. Go in peace and be cured of your affliction."

Cure of the Leper (Mark 1:40–45)
A leper came to him (and kneeling down) begged him and said, "If you wish, you can make me clean." Moved with pity, he stretched out his hand, touched him, and said to him, "I do will it. Be made clean." The leprosy left him immediately, and he was made clean.

Then, warning him sternly, he said to him, "See that you tell no one anything, but go, show yourself to the priest and offer for your cleansing what Moses prescribed; that will be proof for them." The man went away and began to publicize the whole matter. He spread the report abroad so that it was impossible for Jesus to enter town openly. He remained outside in deserted places, and people kept coming to him from everywhere.

Two Blind Men (Matthew 20:29–34)
As Jesus and the disciples left Jericho, a great crowd followed. Two blind men were sitting by the roadside, and when they heard Jesus was passing by, they cried out, "Lord, Son of David, have pity on us!"

The crowd warned them to be silent, but they called out all the more, "Lord, Son of David, have pity on us!"

Jesus stopped and called them and said, "What do you want me to do for you?" They answered him, "Lord, let our eyes be opened." Moved with pity, Jesus touched their eyes. Immediately they received their sight and followed him.

The Good Samaritan (Luke 10:25–27)
There was a scholar of the law who stood up to test him and said, "Teacher, what must I do to inherit eternal life?" Jesus said to him, "What is written in the law? How do you read it?"

He said in reply, "You shall love the Lord, your God, with all your heart, with all your being, with all your strength, and with all your mind, and your neighbor as yourself."

He replied to him, "You have answered correctly; do this and you will live."

But because he wished to justify himself, he said to Jesus, "And who is my neighbor?" Jesus replied, "A man fell victim to robbers as he went down from

Jerusalem to Jericho. They stripped and beat him and went off leaving him half-dead. A priest happened to be going down that road, but when he saw him, he passed by on the opposite side. Likewise, a Levite came to the place, and when he saw him, he passed by on the opposite side. But a Samaritan traveler who came upon him was moved with comparison at the sight.

He approached the victim, poured oil and wine over his wounds and bandaged them. Then he lifted him up on his own animal, took him to an inn and cared for him. The next day he took out two silver coins and gave them to the innkeeper with the instruction, 'Take care of him. If you spend more than what I have given you, I shall repay you on my way back.' Which of these three, in your opinion, was neighbor to the robbers' victim?" He answered, "the one who treated him with mercy." Jesus said to him, "Go and do likewise."

GOSPEL STORIES QUESTIONS ACTIVITY

Name of Parable:
What's going on in the story?
Which values are present in the narrative?
What behavior(s) stands out in the story?
Where do you see examples of this story in our lives today?

REFLECTIVE THINKING PROCESS

Reflective thinking allows you to listen, understand, and share more effectively.

EXPERIENCE—Identify what's going on in the case in terms of...	
Relationship issues:	
Cultural Context:	
Social Milieu:	
Write what you determine into a short summary statement:	
REFLECT— Assess the summary statement in terms of...	
Values:	
CST Principles:	
Scripture Quote:	
Parables:	
RESPOND	
Identify thoughts, insights from the case that influence you as a leader:	
Document what you have learned from this experience:	

SELF-ASSESSMENT
Please respond to the following

1. How was the overall experience of the intensive for you? Please describe.

2. **On a scale of 1–5 please rate your understanding of the Reflective-Thinking Process.**

    1. None   _____
    2. Fair   _____
    3. Good   _____
    4. Very Good   _____
    5. Very Good   _____

3. **What key learning(s) and/or insights have come about for you during the intensive?**

    a. I learned…

    b. An insight for my ministry leadership is…

ABOUT THE AUTHOR

Terrance P. McGuire specializes in organizational, mission, and human development. He has over four decades of ministry leadership experience as a corporate health care executive, educator, and consultant. His experience includes working with religious and lay leadership in Catholic health care, Catholic social services, and other ministry-based organizations.

He presently serves as adjunct faculty at the University of St. Francis in Joliet, IL.

Terry holds a master's degree in Administration from the University of Notre Dame, master's degrees in Pastoral Studies and Spirituality from Loyola University, and doctorates in Education (Ed.D.) from the International Graduate School and Ministry (D.Min.) from the University of St. Mary of the Lake.

Terry is also a Deacon of the Archdiocese of Chicago and ministers at St. Alphonsus Parish in Lemont, IL.

Terry and his wife, Kathleen McGowan, reside in Naperville, IL.

REFERENCES

Chapter 1

Catholic Health Association of the United States. *Framework for Senior Leadership Formation*. Washington, DC: Catholic Health Association of the United States, 2011.

Ed Giganti. "What is Leadership Formation Now." *Health Progress* 85, no. 5 (September-October 2004): 19.

Leonard Doohan. *Spiritual Leadership: The Quest for Integrity*. Mahwah, NJ: Paulist Press, 2007.

National Conference of Catholic Bishops. *Health and Health Care: A Pastoral Letter of the American Catholic Bishops*. Washington, DC: United States Catholic Conference, 1981.

Patricia Talone and Brian P. Smith. "CHA Survey Gauges Formation Effectiveness." *Health Progress* 95, no. 4 (July-August 2014): 47.

Terrance P. McGuire and Kathleen McGowan. *Care for the Caregiver*. Kansas City, MO: Sheed & Ward, 1991.

Chapter 2

John Paul II. *On the Christian Meaning of Human Suffering* (Boston: Pauline Books and Media, 2014), no. 18.

John Welch. *The Carmelite Way*. Mahwah, NJ: Paulist Press, 1996.

Tomas Alvarez. *St. Teresa of Avila: 100 Themes of Her Life and Work*, trans. Kieran Kavanaugh, OCD. Washington, DC: ICS Publications, 2011.

Paul Radzilowski, "The Carmelite Spirituality of John Paul II," *Catholic Exchange* (November 2013),vaccessed February 10, 2017, http://catholicexchange.com/carmelite-spirituality-john-paul-ii.

Chapter 3

Carmelite Sisters for the Aged and Infirm. *The Mother Angeline Society Newsletter* (Summer/Fall 2015): 1.

Joseph Bernardin. *The Gift of Peace*. Chicago: Loyola Press, 1997.

Chapter 4

Herman Hesse. *Stories of Five Decades*. Farrar, Straus, and Giroux, Inc., 1972.

Joseph Luft. *Group Processes: An Introduction to Group Dynamics*. Mayfield Publishing Company, 1984.

Laurence O'Connell, Michael Slubowski, and Terry Weinburger. "Measuring Ministry Formation: Moving Promise into Practice," *Health Progress* 95, no. 4 (July-August 2014): 27.

Patricia Talone and Brian P. Smith. "CHA Survey Gauges Formation Effectiveness." *Health Progress* 95, no. 4 (July-August 2014): 44-50.

Raza Tahreem. "Exploring Transformational and Transactional Leadership Styles," *Queens University IRC*, (November, 2011), accessed February 12, 2017, http://irc.queensu.ca/articles/exploring-transformational-and-transactional-leadership-styles.

Søren Kierkegaard. *Journalen* JJ:167 (1843). *Søren Kierkegaards Skrifter*. Søren Kierkegaard Research Center, Copenhagen, 1997.

Chapter 5

Daniel Sulmasy. *The Healers Calling: A Spirituality for Physicians and Other Health Care Professionals.* New York: Paulist Press, 1997.

Free Dictionary Website, s.v. "cognitive behavior therapy," accessed May 2, 2017. http://medicaldictionary.thefreedictionary.com/cognitive +behavior+therapy.

Free Dictionary Website, s.v. "cognitive restructuring," accessed May 2, 2017. http://medicaldictionary.thefreedictionary.com/cognitive +restructuring.

Herman Hesse. *Siddartha.* Bantam, 1982.

John Shea. *Spirituality and Health Care: Reaching toward a Holistic Future.* Chicago: The Park Ridge Center for the Study of Health, Faith and Ethics, 2000.

Paul W. Pruyser. *The Minister as Diagnostician: Personal Problems in Pastoral Perspective.* Philadelphia, PA: Westminster Press, 1976.

Nick Petrie. *Future Trends in Leadership Development.* Colorado Springs, CO: Center for Leadership Development, 2014.

Wikipedia, s.v. "reflective practice," last modified January 13, 2017, accessed February 12, 2017, https://en.wikipedia.org/wiki/Reflective_practice.

Chapter 6

Catholic Health Association of the United States. *A Shared Statement of Identity for the Catholic Health Ministry.* St. Louis, MO: Catholic Health Association of the United States.

John Paul II. On the Christian Meaning of Human Suffering. Boston: Pauline Books and Media, 2014, no.8

Made in the USA
Columbia, SC
15 August 2019